The
Burnt-Out
Administrator

Carolyn L. Vash, Ph.D., is a psychologist in private consulting practice in Altadena, California. In addition, she serves as a coeditor of the Annual Review of Rehabilitation (Springer Publishing Company, New York), senior associate with the Institute for Information Studies, Washington, D.C., and lecturer in the Schools of Education at the University of Southern California and California State University at Los Angeles. Previously, she served for four years as the chief deputy director of the California State Department of Rehabilitation, and for six years as the chief of vocational services at Rancho Los Amigos Hospital in Downey, California. Severely disabled herself, she has published widely in the areas of the psychology of disability and the civil rights of people who have disabilities.

The
Burnt-Out
Administrator

Carolyn L. Vash, *Ph.D.*

Springer Publishing Company
New York

350
V 333

Springer Publishing Company, Inc.
200 Park Avenue South
New York, N.Y. 10003

80 81 82 83 84 / 10 9 8 7 6 5 4 3 2 1

Library of Congress Cataloging in Publication Data

Vash, Carolyn L
   The burnt-out administrator.

   Includes bibliographical references and index.
   1. Public administration. 2. Organization. 3. Job stress.
4. Executives. I. Title.
JF1411.V37   350   79-14057
ISBN 0-8261-2910-2
ISBN 0-8261-2911-0 pbk.

Printed in the United States of America

To Richard (Husband) and Sibyl (Mother)
who contributed in their own special ways

Contents

Preface ix

Introduction 1

One
Disappearing Rewards 5

Two
Crazymakers: The System 23

Three
Crazymakers: The People 41

Four
The Result 59

Five
Out of the Ashes 77

Bibliography 115

Index 117

Preface

The Burnt-Out Administrator is a survival manual for administrators. The first four chapters, which detail the genesis, process, and result of the problem, came to me in a rush on the eve of my midcareer retirement from the field of human service administration due to a moderate-to-severe case of burn out. Chapter Five, "Out of the Ashes," came more slowly during the following year as a direct result of having written the first four, and experiencing the perennial healer, time. Chapters One through Four take some hard looks and a few swats at various crazymaking phenomena which contribute to administrator burn out. The fifth and final chapter then takes an antinihilistic approach, and suggests a number of ways to reverse the process or avoid it altogether. As a result of having written "Out of the Ashes," I may return to the field of administration one day.

At times it may seem that I swat too hard or, perhaps, unfairly. While I cannot deny the possibility that this is true, it is also true that I have, at one time or another, been a member of nearly every group described in either a kindly or unkindly fashion. I have played the roles of worker, middle manager, top manager, "old guard civil servant," "fresh blood political appointee," "reblessed professional," and many more of the personnel you will meet in the ensuing pages. I must also confess that I have been responsible for creating or supporting some of the policies or practices here exposed as dysfunctional for organizations and the administrators who try to run them. A decade as an administrator and a year of reflection following it have shown me many errors of my own and the system's ways.

Although I have played many roles within a human service agency, I have never administered another kind of operation. Therefore, I must limit my claims of generality to this type of organization. However, a number of administrators in business or other kinds of public fields have reviewed the manuscript and say that the phenomena described apply, often with only minor variations, to their own situations equally well.

It is my hope that the first four chapters will serve as an alerting device to extant administrators, to students, and to others who look forward to future careers in administration. Administering programs and agencies can be exciting and fun for people who are realistically prepared for the frustrations and disappointments that are sure to come. It can be devastating to those who are not. The last chapter is intended to help readers see that while repairing the system might take more than a lifetime, administrators can learn to reap rewards from the faultiest of systems once they acknowledge that the major source, like the major inhibitor, of all rewards lies within.

Carolyn L. Vash

Introduction

There is a great deal of talk, these days, about the phenomenon of burn out among practitioners in the so-called "helping professions." Psychologists, rehabilitation counselors, nurses, social workers, poverty lawyers, school teachers, psychiatrists, and other "people helpers" who are inundated daily by the seemingly insoluble problems of others, appear to just wear out and stop caring. Both the professional journals and the popular press have carried articles on why and how it happens and they generally reflect empathic understanding that too many years of trying to help, heal, or teach those who steadfastly refuse to be helped, healed, or taught can drag on one's spirits and, eventually, extinguish the fires of dedication.

Burn out is not limited to professional people helpers, most of whom work in governmental bureaucracies or private, nonprofit agencies. Their bosses and their bosses' bosses burn out, too. These are the supervisors, middle managers, and top executives who no longer help people directly. Regardless of level, administrators—as a group—have been largely ignored on the subject of burn out. When noticed, it is presumed that they were always dull, jaded, miserly of effort, and detached from the task at hand.

The lack of empathy, such as that felt for practitioners, is not too difficult to understand. Administrators are considered too powerful to love or trust, too successful to pity, and their plight too lacking in the external trappings of drama to be easily romanticized. However, as with the practitioner, there is reason to believe that too many years of trying to manage the unmanageable and change the unchangeable hath power to devastate— leaving a burnt-out shell where once a bright, young, enthusiastic administrator used to be. It seems to be happening more often and faster to better administrators these days.

Should you be one or, perchance, love one, you may agree that they merit concern simply because they are caught in an unfulfilling world of impaired happiness. If not, it is worthwhile to remember that people who become administrators are apt to be among "the brightest and the best" because it takes those qualities to get there. The academic routes through such disciplines as public administration, business administration, and law (fast becoming the standard training for top level government administrators) muster out the least fit. The enormous number of nonadministratively trained administrators who emerge from the professional practitioner ranks to assume management responsibilities are also highly and competitively trained. After these players have entered the world of work there is still more sorting of the less fit from the more fit on the basis of intelligence, creativity, energy, interest, dedication, ambition, toughness, and other survival-related qualities.

What a pity to think of people with attributes such as these either dropping out or ending their days joylessly and mechanically administering whatever is there. Some of the best talent potential of the age may lie dammed up within these souls while the organizations they administer don't work. Whether the organizations were a good idea in the first place is no longer an issue. They have become politico-economic realities on which our whole society, not just the recipients of services, depends. Therefore, we need for them to work. For that to happen, they must be administered by the brightest and the best working at peak effectiveness and efficiency. The conclusion is obvious. Concern for such well-paid, clout-wielding individuals is unavoidable because their sorrows will, ultimately, make sorrows for others. If burnt-out administrators are setting policies that burn out practitioners and sabotage any genuine helpfulness an agency might be to its clients, then the matter merits attention whether they, as a group, win the hearts of the people or not.

Dropping out is a solution not infrequently chosen. Hardly a month goes by without word of another who has vacated a high place in government or the private sector to "do her own thing" or "work with his hands" or whatever offers greater appeal. Others are moving from government to the private sector, or the reverse, with great, high hopes that it will be better—and finding that it is just the same. The acronym for burnt-out administrator—BOA—suggests the constriction and strangulation taking place in both sectors for the same reasons.

The social forces behind the phenomenon of administrator burn out are legion—as multivariate as human nature and as convoluted as the human brain. The purpose of this book is to identify and examine these forces. Some of the major sources of negative emotion for administrators will be described, along with the ways in which these conditions can take the starch out of even the strongest.

Chapter One, *Disappearing Rewards*, illustrates how administrators no longer have either the power or autonomy attributed to them. It explains the mechanisms by which the rewards are being lost, and describes how the realization comes —sometimes in spurts and sometimes in volleys—to administrators trying to do their work, day by day.

Chapters Two and Three, *Crazymakers: The System* and *Crazymakers: The People*, are almost self-explanatory. The assignment of specific phenomena to one chapter or the other is sometimes clear-cut and sometimes arbitrary. It is difficult to separate the system from the people who create and manifest it. Many of the "system" phenomena described were introduced to correct problems seen at other levels by other viewers. Many of the "people" phenomena are little more than human nature at its most troublesome; that is, when disparate natures must interact toward a common goal.

Chapter Four, *The Result*, shows the net effect of all of the multifarious pressures on the administrator's body, mind, and spirit. Throughout, in reading about these phenomena, it is important to keep in mind that although they are necessarily presented one by one, to the administrator to whom they are happening, they are all going on at the same time. It is this fact that overwhelms and devastates. Living in the center of the cyclone, with no safe ground anywhere and in a chronic state of "information overload" and "psychological crowding," leads inexorably to physiological and behavioral deterioration among even the strongest and most resourceful human beings—just as physical crowding has been shown to do with lower species.

If the book ended here, the effect could be mortally depressing. Happily, however, there is another view. Chapter Five, *Out of the Ashes*, presents that more hopeful perspective. Having seen what happens to administrators to dampen their fervor and dull their sensitivities, the next step is to generate ways to either improve conditions or render the administrator less vulnerable to such soul-eroding effects. It is the thesis of this final chapter that having looked and laughed at an incredible welter of foolishly wasted efforts and spurious concerns, and having reappraised fully the meaning of "power" and what it is in this life that may actually matter, a formerly burnt-out administrator could conceivably be free to do the best administrative job of a lifetime, and experience singular enjoyment while doing so.

Chapter 1

Disappearing Rewards

Two rewards which used to make all of the responsibilities and heartaches of administrative work worthwhile were the power and autonomy that went with the job. Administrators could frequently make happen what they believed should happen in the way they wanted it to happen. They were sufficiently free from supervisory constraints to indulge their creative abilities or their egotistical whims or both. Because they took responsibility for their own mistakes, they were free to make them and pay the consequences. When a hunch or strategy paid off with positive results, the prospect of a raise or a promotion existed and could tantalize. The freedom to make decisions, some of which involved considerable risks, was a cardinal attribute of the profession. Things have changed.

There is now a burgeoning constellation of forces, all interacting at once, which reduce, sometimes annihilate, the degree of creative control an administrator may enjoy. Workers from all occupational classes are unionizing. Funding shortages every-where grow worse, yearly. Demands such as those for affirma-tive action, consumer involvement, and accountability keeping take their toll. When there is high unemployment, people cling to their jobs, even if they are not good at them, and the prob-lems associated with firing incompetent workers worsen. It is trying to deal with all of these situations, and many more, and all at once, that immobilizes the administrator's ability to try the new, the experimental, the creative.

During high school or college years, some professor or guidance counselor probably asked each future administrator to complete a form which included rank ordering a list of job re-wards according to one's own values. These lists contain items such as: *security, opportunities for promotion, compatible co-workers, freedom to use own initiative, good working condi-tions, clear instructions, friendly supervisors, high salary,* and *opportunity for creative expression.* The students headed for blue collar jobs usually ranked items such as: *high salary, se-curity,* and *good working conditions* highest. Students headed for white collar jobs tended to place the highest value on: *free-dom to use own initiative, opportunities for creative expres-sion,* and *opportunities for promotion.* The latter group, obviously, included those who later became administrators.

Although unions serve an extremely valuable social pur-pose, they may be unbearably frustrating to the administrator. A reasonable, operational definition of "frustration" might be: "the attempt, by an administrator, to express his or her creativ-ity with one or more union representatives looking on." At close observation one tends to be inhibited from doing what comes naturally. The bargaining team offers help to ensure that any directives forthcoming will be accepted by the troops. One can be sure that if the help offered is not incorporated, the troops will find the directive unacceptable. (Sometimes, the communication within an organization is excellent. It has taken professionals a long time to become dissatisfied enough to orga-nize, but now that they are doing so, they are proving that they know how to take care of people, including themselves.)

An administrator may feel certain that a proposed approach would work and would also improve the quality of worklife for employees if they would give it a chance. Administrators are not callous to the needs of workers. After all, their entire training and work backgrounds have been permeated with the importance of high worker morale, for its own sake as well as for the sake of production. Few managers strive to develop an unhappy workforce. But the continual disappointments of seeing creative blossoms nipped in the bud by a group purporting to represent that workforce does make it progressively harder to go on caring whether morale remains high; yet one must. It's a bind.

Unfortunately, if the unions don't checkmate your operation, the control agencies will. Control agencies are here construed as whatever entities pass laws, promulgate regulations, or otherwise watch over you to ensure compliance with something or other. What "the feds" are to state programs, the Congress is to "the feds." Public or private, large or small, the effect on the service delivery agencies and their administrators is about the same. Every time a creative administrator comes up with a fresh, new idea which might work, there is some offbeat element in it that has been defined as a "no-no" at some level; and any efforts to implement the plan will be met with charges of noncompliance.

At the extreme, government administrators are sometimes caught between conflicting local and federal laws. The California voters recently defeated an attempt by the state legislature to force state administrators to follow state laws even though they believed them to be in conflict with federal statutes. Blessed be the voters, who saved a number of administrators from having to decide whether to go to state versus federal prison.

Depending on the intensity of the need for creative expression and the level of frustration tolerance, and after being thus trapped or stung for the third or three-hundredth time, the administrator begins to notice that the fires of imagination have become a little hard to ignite.

Whatever Happened to Management Prerogatives?

As an illustration of the problem, a newly formed union of professional workers in state government, in 1976, asked for a meet-and-confer with top management of the agency for which most of the membership worked. Management duly agreed to meet-and-confer on most of the points listed, but declined to discuss certain others—indicating decisions there fell within the purview of "management prerogatives." The union did not accept this and grieved the matter before the state's personnel agency. Weeks passed; eventually, a decision descended with the governor's blessing.

More technical and less concise, it said, in essence, "management *has* no prerogatives." It made clear that management would meet-and-confer on any topic on which a union wished to meet-and-confer. There would be no "king's X" areas where management might ignore the opinions and feelings of the workers, even though it would ultimately bear the burden of blame if things went wrong. It was reasoned that punishing the administrator after the fact would not help the worker who suffered harm while a prerogative was being carried out. In short, management would be *prevented* from making mistakes, not punished for having made them. That decision took considerable dignity from being in the post of an administrator.

Workers have long known what it does to them when management attempts to render errors impossible by routinizing and manualizing what should be left to professional prerogative or plain common sense. It demoralizes them. Management has now begun to roast on the same spit, and the workers have nearly wriggled off. Ironically, the brightest and the best among the union workers will someday be promoted into management positions and into the unfulfilling roles they helped to create. That may give a few extant administrators a moment of satisfaction.

Almost all groups of professional workers are unionizing now, including the last holdouts who once abjured it as beneath their professional station. Why? Have work organizations become more corrupt or managers less competent, ethical, or fair, forcing workers to protect themselves against new dangers? Probably not. What seems to be happening is an outrageously escalating demand for *fairness* which is utterly against all reasonable odds in a world where fairness to one so often infringes upon the perceived rights of another. It has aptly been labeled "the expectation explosion." Born in the sixties, it is a phenomenon which grows relentlessly larger and stronger. We have come to expect much, and we are devastated and vindictive when our expectations are not met. When we are hurt, someone other than ourselves must pay. If not, the unfairness of it all is intolerable. We file lawsuits and grievances, rant and rave, and have heart attacks and strokes, all in the course of demanding that the world treat us fairly.

The symbol of the legal profession is the scales of justice. Like any other, this noble conception becomes warped and destructive when people with limited capacities for seeing scope and context clutch at it as the only solution to every problem. You don't turn the other cheek when you're keeping an eye on the scales. It may not be a coincidence that the number of lawyers in management and the volume of employee grievances are rising together. Lawyer administrators may foster legalistic solutions to employee problems in ways so subtle even they don't recognize them. It can happen through managerial rhetoric influenced by the language and concepts of their profession as well as by direct example. Since many are top level political appointees rather than civil servants in the public sector, their styles have high visibility and are likely to be copied.

There are agencies where labor, management, and the clientele would all agree that too much of the energy expended in the organization is being channeled into processing claims and counterclaims among employees, or between employees and clients, with too little residual going into actual services for the clientele. In addition to the unions striving to wrest the remaining shreds of autonomy from management while the latter clutches, disbelieving, as these slip away, there are other, possibly even bigger, internal time and energy consumers in many organizations. One of them has the nonspecific and increasingly ironic label of "affirmative action."

The Affirmative Action Bomb

The affirmative action bomb fell on management in the early nineteen seventies. Also a child of the sixties, it was construed as a means for bringing that decade's unrest to an end. Equal employment opportunity would be mandated, and soon the class distinctions between white and nonwhite would disappear. The shock of liberal administrators, when they realized that to act on moral principles they fully endorsed meant hiring some people less competent than others available to carry out their lives' dedications, was both tragic and comical. The more bigoted administrators suffered less. They were only doing what the government was forcing them to do. They had no inner turmoil to reconcile. The others tried to assure themselves that their convictions that there were few qualified minority candidates for professional jobs reflected the universities' failures to train sufficient numbers, not prejudicial attitudes on their parts.

A middle manager in the field of rehabilitation services put it this way:

> I do believe in what the affirmative action program is all about. I know that you can and must legislate morality. Gradualism isn't good enough. But right now, I've got a problem! I believe in their (the affirmative action office) cause, but they don't give a damn about mine. I want to get people with *disabilities* into jobs, and they deserve a break just as much as minorities. Many of them *are* minorities. Right now I am being pressured—no, let's be honest, I'm being threatened—to hire the only minority applicant who interviewed for a vacancy I am trying to fill. This guy actually dozed off in the interview! If I have to hire him, and summarily reject a white candidate whom I know could do a good job because he did student field work here, then there is a whole caseload of clients who aren't going to get very much help around here. They (top management) keep subtly suggesting that I must have developed a friendship with this former student and, not so subtly, bring up the fact that the new annual performance evaluation forms for administrative personnel include "affirmative action" as a rating category. Well, I'm not going to hire a minority applicant who is incompetent just to keep from getting

marked down. This is no straw man you know. Other department heads are doing just that. They can fire me for all I care. I can find better things to do than try to sail a ship which I know has been scuttled.

That was in 1972. Today, that administrator's cause célèbre has been added to the growing list of "protected populations" for which employers must set hiring goals. In the meantime, the administrator quoted has moved up into top management. How does she feel now about affirmative action programs?

Well, it's certainly not the same kind of problem it was. Most of the jobs for which we hire require at least a bachelor's degree and a few require the doctorate. The universities are training some minority people in the fields in which we hire. I can always find qualified minority applicants at the bachelor's level and often at the master's. It is still too early to find many with doctorates, but in a few years that won't be a problem. It sure is nice to have disabled folks on the list! But you know, now I'm being just as obnoxious to other employers, trying to get them to hire workers with disabilities, as I thought the minority advocates were being a few years ago. Like them, I find myself suspecting prejudice against people with disabilities whenever someone questions whether they can find a qualified disabled widget maker or whatever. However, in the cool light of reason, it doesn't take a statistician to figure out that on a pure probability basis, the chances of finding a qualified *anything* are less if you are recruiting from the ten percent (disabled or other minority) rather than the ninety percent (ablebodied or other majority) pool of potential workers.

The problems with affirmative action hiring are gradually being outgrown. I say *gradually* because minority college graduates are often not the academic peers of majority graduates. They were admitted with lesser qualifications, and, as a part-time prof, I can tell you it's true that they are frequently graded less stringently, all in the interest of a good cause. Right though it be, their performance deficits, when they come to work, are real and will not disappear in one generation. Maybe in two or three.

Now the big problem has shifted from initial hiring to promotions. As a recent example for me, do you have any idea how frus-

trating it can be to have an outstandingly competent white female
candidate for a middle management vacancy, and to feel sure you
are on the side of the angels if you promote her, only to be told
that you must give the position to an admittedly mediocre male
administrator with a Spanish surname? The top man, it seems,
is concerned only about affirmative action for "Chicanos" this
year. This happened in spite of the fact that I was farther from
meeting promotional goals for women than for people with Spanish
surnames.

This is an interesting thing that is happening. If a conservative
administration engaged in the cronyism and favoritism to special
interest groups that liberal administrations are doing under the
banner of affirmative action, the charges of "unconstitutional"
would be deafening. Everyone knows that what is going on now is
unconstitutional, but the most you hear is embarrassed, muffled
mutters. Isn't that fascinating? The oppressed become the oppres-
sors. Will it ever change? Probably not.

Just as the problems in initial hiring have given way to
problems regarding whom to promote, so will the latter eventually be eased by truly equal educational opportunities and
increased appreciation of equivalent, if not equal, talents across
the various ethnic groups. That happy prospect for the future
does not, however, erase the fact that at present, the problems
are maddening and contribute substantially to burning out
administrators who cannot let go of their own goals temporarily
to focus on accomplishing different ones. The controversial
Bakke decision and related lower court decisions which purport
to disallow "reverse discrimination" as a result of affirmative
action programs have made their administration more, not less,
difficult. The language in these decisions is so lacking in internal
consistency that the administrator has no basis for predicting
the "safe" way to go.

Pity the poor administrators. About one-third of their
autonomy has been depleted by the unions, and another third
by the office of affirmative action. That would leave one-third
for themselves except for yet another group who is moving in
fast to envelope the remaining portion. This multitudinous
group is often spoken of in the singular as The Consumer.

Consumerism and the Hard Knocks
Diploma Mill

Market research has long been part of the organizational milieu in industries which manufacture and
distribute products. In the private sector of competitive free
enterprise, organizations that dispense services have joined the
product manufacturers in attempting to increase customer satisfaction and, therefore, sales. However, in both the public and
private nonprofit sectors of human service delivery, "the customer is always right" has been an alien phrase. In fact, its very
opposite has often appeared to reflect the guiding principle of
the agencies which deal out education, health, employment,
welfare, and other social services. The direct service workers are
generally professionals with college degrees, sometimes ad-
vanced ones. These workers do not take kindly to the notion
that they may not know better than the clients what clients
need. After all, they got college degrees in what it is that clients
need. The administrators above them typically came up from
the ranks of the same professions and share the same mystique.
At the same time, because these services are frequently tax supported, there is great and vocal concern about "duplication of
services," but no concern whatsoever about the existence of
monopolies. As a result, most of these service agencies are the
only game in town and if the client isn't satisfied, it really
doesn't matter because there is nowhere else to go anyway. For
these reasons and possibly others, there has been a long history
of no market research in the area of human services.

Everything is changing all at once. Ralph Nader and company are probing relentlessly into these sacrosanct areas. In the
public sector, a service-recipient constituency learned several
years ago that testifying before Congressional committees
works, and they have been utilizing this knowledge on a regular
basis ever since. Moreover, they are playing a "for keeps" ver-
sion of musical chairs with the professional experts in which
they simply grab the chairs before the sheltered, bemused professionals know what is happening. Central to this is a new
mentality, embodied in a "peer helper" movement, which is

taking hold. The primary theme is that in order to truly understand and be helpful to (some particular group of people) one must have personally experienced their situation. "It takes one to know one" is no longer a joke. Coping strategies are still developing.

First, the experts and their organizations created consumer advisory committees as palliative window dressing, a gesture rich with overtones of noblesse oblige. Well, they let the camel get its nose inside the tent. Despite the Carter administration's roll back on advisory committees, many have taken hold and will continue to advise whether their advice is wanted or not. Some such committees are beginning to do to public agencies what Nader et al. are doing to private business—and more. They not only demand that a better service be delivered, they demand that their own kind be hired to deliver it.

Meanwhile, the managers of such beleaguered organizations are trying to take care of business while their threatened, angry staff have little time to do likewise after long hours of mutual reassurance about the security of their jobs. When management deigns to insist that they get the work out, they, instead, demand that management offer them protection against their jobs being sublet to "consumer types" who, somehow, have greater political access to the bosses than they do. It is painful to learn that the years of effort, denial, and discipline it took to get a college degree were wasted. The degree is considered relatively worthless in comparison with the education gained adventitiously by consumers of services in the school of hard knocks. Staff with crushed egos and threatened pocketbooks can be counted on to make life hell for the administrator.

An administrator who is still young put it this way:

> I guess my management style is just too outmoded to fit today's climate. I just can't see expending all of my energy trying to meet the demands of the employees, primarily, and, secondarily, those of a handful of militant, vocal consumers who probably represent no one but themselves. I'm old-fashioned enough to think that some of the effort ought to be directed into meeting the needs of the great mass of consumers, our clients. Frankly, it's just no fun anymore.

He paused and then continued musing:

> You know, I used to feel that our staff was a real *team*. All of us seemed to be pulling together toward the same goal of really helping the clients put their lives together. But it's not that way anymore. It seems like everyone is out for "me first" and to hell with the clients! The old sense of camaraderie and teamwork is gone, and I'm not exactly sure what happened to it.

The Unteam

When is a team not a team? When the members make no choices about joining or staying. It is then an adventitious collection of individuals, each of whom got there by a different route and made no commitment to being on a team with any other member. In the work situation just described, there was probably no commitment to group membership at all. Most likely, a commitment was made to doing a particular kind of job. Incidental to that, the job existed within an organization which happened to have other employees who, *en toto* or in clusters, were viewed *by someone else* as one or more "teams."

Unteams in work situations stay together for a number of reasons, virtually all of which devolve upon real or perceived lack of occupational mobility. If the members saw themselves as free to leave, they almost certainly would because such groups offer little hope for fulfillment. It is stressful to maintain the pretense of a team when, in fact, there is competition and isolationism.

Democratic or not, if an administrator is to have a functioning team of workers who pull together toward the same goal with complementary and compatible styles, then that administrator must be able to select the team members with group interactions in mind. Characteristics of individual temperament must be considered, not as specifics, but how these might add to or detract from the group. Whether the new employee's philosophy is compatible with the prevailing philosophy of the team is of critical importance. However, there is very little allowance for the use of such flexibility and intuition in personnel selection in private agencies, and it is next to impossible in civil service hiring. A job applicant who brought a grievance complaint of being rejected solely because of personality incompatibility with team incumbents would almost certainly win his or her case. Yet, the person's presence could undermine the team's effectiveness. Thus, the problem begins with constraints imposed upon selection.

Once the error of selection has been made, it is almost impossible to correct because of the extreme difficulty entailed in trying to terminate an employee who is unwilling to relinquish a job. Whether the worker is potentially capable but poorly placed, or blatantly incompetent for any possible job in the organization, if s/he doesn't want to budge, the chances are, s/he won't. The problem is most difficult under civil service rules. So much prior, written documentation is required that the process of obtaining it tends to do two highly undesirable things: it ensures the destruction of any vestiges of a workable relationship between documentor and documentee, and it nudges both toward the brink of chronic paranoid thinking.

While it may be a bit less difficult to terminate an incompetent employee in the private sector, the growing threats of complaints to fair employment practice and equal employment opportunity monitoring agencies are beginning to block such terminations as effectively as civil service rules have done for years. Unions in both the public and private sectors will fight just as hard for the retention of an incompetent employee as for an effective one who is being mistreated. Naturally, with today's high rates of unemployment, workers are clinging tenaciously to their jobs; and their advocacy groups must do battle for all to maintain political viability.

The problem is further compounded by the fact that many colleges and universities have produced more would-be practitioners for certain fields than the market can absorb. Some are fully aware that they are glutting the market, but continue to train at maximum program capacity (relaxing admission standards, when necessary) to avoid cutting back instruction staff.

Professors are clinging tenaciously to their jobs, too. This generates untold numbers of graduates who grab whatever job they can find in their fields, hoping to locate a more suitable position later on. Unfortunately, they may find that it takes months or even years to do so. By then, the "team" they have graced with their semipresence may have a great deal to recover from.

The final insult to a functioning team comes from accountability systems which foster competition among employees. For example, if you get comparative credit as an individual for every job placement you effect, you are likely to guard your sources rather than share them with colleagues when their clients need leads. More will be said about accountability systems later.

In the absence of a true team, it is unlikely that positive changes in a service delivery system can be implemented. Progressive efforts may be initiated, but without team support, they are destined to die aborning. Thus, the bright and shiny ideals of new administrators to serve as agents for change may tarnish quickly. As will be seen, more than a simple lack of teamship is responsible.

The Big Change Agent Disillusion

Is there an administrator alive who has not attended one of those four-day courses designed to make managers out of people who probably should have been almost anything else? If not a four-day, then at least a three- or two-day. The trainers are entertaining and stimulating with their clever packages of easy-to-remember (or so it seems at the time) explanations of the entire managerial cosmos. Dichotomies, trichotomies, slogans, grids, and graphs are presented in rooms resplendent with endlessly flipping easel charts.

A few years ago the favorite catchword of the wonder-course circuit was "changeagent." Top executives, middle managers, supervisors, and others were enjoined to learn how they could be agents of change. It was incredibly popular and had an almost religious appeal. The rhetoric suggested that administrators were instruments (agents) of a higher power which could be channeled through them—thereby relieving them of responsibility for claiming power for themselves and yet promising the rewards of heaven. In the main, the fascination came and went within five years. It came because administrators needed desperately to believe they had some control, the power to effect some of the changes they wanted to see. It went because it became clear that however desperately it might have been wanted, it was illusory. The power lay elsewhere. Several of its lodging places have already been discussed. The wonder-course trainers began making statements such as, "But you must never forget, the power in an organization is always at the bottom."

Nonetheless, the people at the bottom behave as if they believed it to be at the top. The people at the top sense exactly where it is but are generally unable to articulate it clearly. They learn quickly that where the ability to sabotage management directives lies, there also lies the power. Sabotage comes in many varieties. "Malicious compliance" is a favorite in government agencies because so many of them are peopled by long-term civil servants "led" briefly by short-term political appointees. Malicious compliance occurs when veteran subordinates, who know better, comply with a disastrous directive from a new boss, who doesn't know at all, just to watch the walls come tumbling down. A buddy would send up a warning flare.

The trainers revealed that the avoidance of malicious compliance and other forms of programmatic sabotage depends on "participatory management." Then it often turned out that all the talk about change agentry was just another way of getting administrators to attend another course on that well-worn subject. Unfortunately, a lecture on democracy-in-action may not be exactly what you need when you're in the middle of a revolution. Administrator as agent of change? Many feel much more the pawn of changes imposed upon them. One who is remarkably able to implement changes in the face of great opposition acknowledges both his success and his discomfort. He likens his world to the jaws of a vice. Increasingly militant workers are pressing hard from one direction and pressing just as relentlessly from the other are four major control entities (the federal umbrella agency, the state legislature, the state personnel agency, and the state finance agency) which generate new laws, policies, regulations, accounting procedures, and other nonproduction demands which must, somehow, come out of production time.

In spite of it all, many managers can respond as fast as a central office can demand. They don't resist change, they love it. They are not reactionary and future shocked, they are forward looking and eager to implement changes they have taken the trouble to identify as needed. But they are being blocked. On one side of the vise it is by subordinates who are motivated mainly to test their developing muscle rather than any real objections to proposed changes. On the other side, it is by a hopelessly entangled network of sometimes overlapping, sometimes conflicting, external demands which are frequently monitored by inflexible people. As noted earlier, one such demand has been a source of dissension among workers and between workers and management. It is the demand to document and demonstrate accountability.

The Age of Accountability

Some administrators can recall the days before the term "accountability" became the hottest linguistic property in the business. They will remember when "responsibility" was The Word, usually coupled with "authority." You weren't supposed to have the former without an equal amount of the latter. Now you are not supposed to have a job at all unless you have some given, readily measurable amount of accountability. The measures do not have to make sense to the consumers or the employees, but they do have to fit the data systems of the control agencies. The problem is, the process tends to grow until it has consumed a significant part of one's eight-hour work day. No matter what your vocational predilections might have been when you thought you chose a career, your work is destined to become accounting: for time expenditures and, theoretically, accomplishments, should you finish documenting previous activities in time.

One does not run a happy organization when it is comprised of people doing little of what they thought the job entailed, a great deal of tallying whatever they had time to do, and then deciding, along with their supervisors, whether it was enough. The supervisors are doing the same thing with *their* supervisors. It is generally unclear what, if any, sanctions are to be applied if the sum total output is not considered enough. Punishment comes equally to all, regardless of quality and quantity of output, in the form of chronic anxiety lest somebody-up-there decided that production is insufficient and do *something.*

Quantity of output is emphasized simply because it is so much harder to measure quality, especially in the production of services. For example, if an employment service puts workers into 100,000 jobs during a given period of time, no one asks whether the 100,000 points they credited to themselves includes 30,000 jobs which had to be refilled and, perhaps, refilled again because the match between worker and job demands was so poorly made. Similarly, no one asks whether the job placements which "stick" do so because the worker is well placed, or because the worker is economically trapped. One hundred thousand points is 100,000 points, whether you make it the easy way or the hard way, but the hard way generally takes longer. Once the control agencies have grown used to large numbers, the service agency that wants to do a quality job at some necessary expense in numbers will be threatened with extinction if it tries to do so.

At the same time, workers are pushing back hard against all efforts to hold them accountable for quantitative indices of production. The impetus of the counterthrust increases with the paper-work demands of accountability systems which prevent them from accomplishing enough to impress anyone anyway. They know that the present cannot compare favorably with the past for two reasons. Funding falls ever shorter of keeping up with the inflationary spiral, creating an effective reduction in funds available; and no matter how recent the past comparison base, it always consumed a little less time in accountability paper work than the present.

"Paper work" is an older term than "accountability," but

it has long been the tangible manifestation of trying to hold individuals or groups accountable. "Paper work" is also an older term than "program evaluation," but it is the tangible manifestation of that phenomenon as well. Program evaluation is a systematic way of measuring what everyone in the organization has been doing—within the limits of present methodology, of course—so that the whole and each individual, unit, or other subdivision can be held accountable for what they did or did not do. It is exceedingly easy for workers to sabotage any program evaluation system simply by supplying meaningless numbers that make them seem to comply with it. This induces an exquisite frustration in the administrator who may know or sense that it is happening and yet be unable to do anything about it.

"Plan" is an even older term than "paper work," but when juxtaposed with "program evaluation" in work organizations, it takes on new meaning. A plan is a document wherein one records what one intends to do. This is done in simple, concrete, measurable terms, from the gross objectives to their most miniscule subparts, so that evaluators can tell, later on, whether it was done. This means that someone must turn the words in the plan into numbers.

It is a great deal easier to turn, "I plan to achieve 100 job placements" into a number than it is to thus translate, "I plan to place the maximum possible number of people in jobs which will use their talents, be rewarding to them, offer decent potential for promotion, and pay no less than their previous jobs." The latter exceeds the capabilities of most computers and their programmers as well. It is, of course, the computer which has brought the entire situation about. There must be a Parkinson's Law which governs the endlessly expanding use of computers. Surely, a general principle of the technological universe in which we find both ourselves and computers is, "If we *can* do it, we *do* do it." Afterward, some people wonder how they ever got along before. They are happier than those who remember getting along perfectly well.

Some even remember when *trust* was considered an important variable influencing both the workers' output and the bosses' perceptions of it. The very existence of elaborate, computerized planning-evaluation-accountability systems constitutes and promulgates a tidal wave of nontrust. It floods down from the top with new waves spurting out at each craggy step of the organization. The workers feel bad because they are not trusted, nervous because they are being monitored, and mad because the variables on which they are being monitored are not relevant to the provision of good services. As a result, they are not very much fun for administrators to orchestrate.

Who created the monster? How did this thing come about? In querying administrators for their opinions, the answers received are but two. The vast majority say, "*They* have! The control agencies have done it!" But a quiet, even hushed, minority responds in a small, tentative voice, "The control agencies started it, but we went along, and I think we may have done it to ourselves!"

Chapter 2

Crazymakers: The System

In case someone should imagine that a crazymaker is something other than the obvious, it is not. A crazymaker is something which, by its very nature, tends to make people crazy. The double bind and the mixed message are prototypic crazymakers. There are many theories about how schizophrenics come to be schizophrenics, and one thing on which there is some agreement is that their folks, especially their mothers, put them in many double binds and gave them a number of mixed messages. Parents who do this are called "schizophrenogenic." In case "double bind" and "mixed message" require definition, with the former you are damned if you don't and damned if you do. The latter is exemplified by the mother who tells her child "I love you," but seems to have her fists clenched while saying it.

Not unlike the schizophrenogenic home environment, there are plenty of double binds and mixed messages in work

organizations. There is an abundant supply of other available
crazymakers, too. This chapter and the next explore a number
of them. Whereas the next chapter covers matters relating
primarily to individuals and positions in organizations, this one
focuses on issues that are relatively more tied to organizational
structure and dynamics. It begins with the deadliest one of all.

The Security Trap

Alan Watts wrote a wonderful book in 1951 en-
titled *The Wisdom of Insecurity.* In it, he explored
the "law of reverse effort" which governs such perverse effects
as: when you try to stay on the surface of the water, you sink;
but when you try to sink, you float. Watts maintained that the
overwhelming sense of insecurity which engulfs so many of us is
the direct result of trying so hard to be secure. His juxtaposition
of the words "wisdom" and "insecurity" seemed to fly in the
face of reason. The American ideal is better reflected in the television commercials that show how unerringly the hero provided
for security in the future—for himself, his wife, and his children
—and the tragedies that befall the poor fool who fails to plan
ahead. Such commercials advertise either savings and loan or
insurance companies, both of which trade in getting people to
save their money today in order to have some to spend on a
distant tomorrow.

What is security? At one level of meaning, it is a functional
delusion we nurture; a pathetic hope for a guarantee that if
we do everything in the right way, and there is always someone
around to tell us what that is, then nothing will ever go wrong.
That level of meaning may rather easily be recognized as all too
human but unrealistic. One remembers Job, impeccable, old
Job, and how many guarantees he got. However, at another
level of meaning, "security" translates rather simply as "future
money." Security as future money, and not too much less than
one has grown used to, is a hard one to put down. Furthermore,
almost no one is trying.

Company retirement plans are among the most cost-effective future money plans existing. As a result, many people hold jobs of which they have long since grown weary solely because they offer the best future money alternative available. This is as true in human service organizations as anywhere else. If today's professionals rank ordered that "job reward" list when they were young, they probably abjured security in favor of opportunities for creative expression. Time does its work, however, and the persistent, dominant, practical, societal brainwash gets to a number of them and the lofty ideals collapse. They do not even work for their current salary. If they were that hedonistically in tune with the here and now, they might be easier to reach. But they are in a state of suspended animation where today barely exists except as a memory-in-the-making when the all important future, with its perfectly adequate money supply, arrives.

Illustrating the inseparability of system from people variables, this is most likely to happen to people who recoil from the anxiety of frequent (or even infrequent) job changes and, thus, afix themselves to a secure job with the tenacity of a barnacle clinging to the underside of a ship. Sometimes they fantasize about leaving, someday, for a different kind of work experience, but decide that their family obligations make this impossible. Sometimes the family leaves first, blowing their cover. Occasionally, such a jab to the lifestyle may jolt the person out of the rut. For the ingrained, however, there is a period of floundering, followed by the hasty construction of a new set of binding obligations.

The administrator frequently wants and needs to reach these people because they are chronically out of tune on the job. Not quite incompetent enough to fire, their timing is wrong and finesse is lacking. It is particularly frustrating because one senses that the same individual might come alive in a new job in a different setting. But no one will ever know, for sure, because it is too expensive, in the imaginary tender of future money, to abandon one retirement program and enter another. Naturally, this happens most often to workers who have lived at least half of their work life—who have had all of the promotions they are going to have, or have even slipped back a bit. Unfortunately, however, this is not always the case. There is another hook on this claw that snags younger workers, too. At this stage, it has as much to do with dreams of glory as with future money. It is the beginning of . . . .

The Long, Narrow, Windowless, Vertical Tunnel

You know what tunnel that is, don't you? It is the promotional channel offered by certain work organizations, prototypic of which is the civil service system. To protect civil servants who are already in the system from losing what few promotional opportunities there are (compared with the numbers of workers at the entry level), rules are created which prohibit jobs at supervisory, middle management, and some of the top management levels from being filled by outsiders. The positions are reserved for those who are paying their dues by climbing up the hierarchy from the bottom. Opportunities designated "promotional only" ensure that one's only competitors will be others who, like oneself, have stuck with the system. As illustrated earlier, sticking with the system may reflect traits which are less than endearing to the topmost administrator, who is likely to be a politically appointed outsider. While it may reflect dedication and competence, it may also reflect inordinate preoccupation with future income, fears of confronting job examinations and interviews on unfamiliar territory, and/or general inertia. All of this tends to guarantee that the competition for promotions will be reasonable. There will be no unpleasant surprises like supercompetent candidates discovered outside. This arrangement is known as "the civil service merit system."

Any government agency director who has ever tried to put the best available people into the highest agency positions suspects that the people with the most merit were in some other system at the time. Again, it is a simple matter of probabilities. With a pool of, say, a dozen managers to choose from within an agency, and a pool of thousands outside, where do you think the probabilities are best for finding a topnotch person to fill a job? But that choice is not available because the system (we, the people) has chosen to protect the security of incumbent employees rather than the recipients of the work they do. It is true that some terrible wrongs were committed against individual workers before laws, regulations, and rules were created to protect them. The price paid, unfortunately, is that the quality of work, in a number of areas, has been going down, down, down ever since.

For the ambitious job seeker the picture is this. With a few exceptions (the so-called "exempt" positions for which elected officials can hire whom they please), there is only one way to obtain a high level, responsible, prestigious, powerful position in the civil service. You start at the bottom and climb your way, laboriously and systematically, with no short circuiting or double jumping, to the top. The chances are that by the time you get there you will be too tired, and you will certainly be too indoctrinated, to do anything new and unusual. That may be part of the design.

This has some unfortunate consequences for an organization. These are felt keenly by administrators who are appointed to the exempt, uppermost management positions. To begin with the obvious, you know of people outside who could do certain jobs magnificently, but you cannot touch them. Although no one within the house shows genuine interest in a given task to be done, someone will take it if it means a promotion. You give them the assignment and pray for the best.

Second, and this one is both subtle and insidious, the workers within the system are likely to be low risk takers. The civil service tends to attract people who prefer to avoid the risks of less secure employment, and their risk-avoidance is nurtured by the system once they are in it. Many are there because of the nature of the system rather than in spite of it. However, to illustrate by analogy, if you happen to be crippled, you don't want someone to marry you because of that fact. You would suspect dangerous power needs, or kinkiness. You want someone to marry you in spite of your disability, demonstrating that love conquers all, including whatever esthetic or functional liabilities it presents. Similarly, when you know you are running an organization which is crippled by any number of dysfunctional policies and unwelcome constraints, you don't particularly want employees who are attracted to those deformations. The last thing you want if you are administering anything that needs to be improved is a house filled with low risk takers. Admittedly, you don't want all high risk takers, either; you could have more creative chaos than any sane administrator would care to endure. But you must have high risk takers in some key positions if you hope to generate anything other than business-as-usual in the limited time that you have. The problem is additionally confounded by the fact that you, if you are an exempt appointee, are likely to be a high risk taker yourself. If you were not, you would not have accepted a position which is certain to self-destruct within a relatively short period of time and which offers no transfer rights or security of any kind. Thus, a very basic personality conflict, and its resulting communication impediments, is added to a relationship which is bound to be somewhat tension filled, even for more compatible temperaments. Your high risk adventures will drive them bananas, and their low risk conservatism will drive you insane.

Third, and closely related, there is a very strong tendency for the workers in the organization to think very much alike. Part of this may stem from homogeneous temperaments. After all, they did make similar decisions about their life's work. But more important, they have been "living" together, day after day, some of them for a long, long time, in a very small house which has only one door and keeps its windows shut. As a result, they develop a highly cohesive, if not downright incestuous, tightly closed in-group which is thoroughly versed in "the agency way" and extremely hostile to outsiders with their different approaches and ideas. "Promotional-only" isolationism breeds xenophobia. The appointed administrator comes in as an unwelcome overseer regardless of personal qualities. The very existence of the exempt position challenges firmly held beliefs that no outsider can function appropriately, or offer relevant ideas, in the absense of some critical mass of experience in the same agency. This is a very important fiction to maintain. It is integral to the rationale for foreclosing on all outsiders who might want to compete for those "promotional only" jobs. Once you admit that someone from the outside, including an appointed director, could put a different kind of experience to good use in the agency, then you have let the camel get its nose inside the tent. The next thing you know, they will be crossing out "promotional only" and writing in "open examination" on a job test you intend to take.

The tunnel is long and narrow, and the windows have been boarded up tightly to guard against midlevel invasion; but the existence of exempt positions leaves it open at the top. As is undoubtedly evident by now, no administrator addicted to being thought well of should ever accept such an appointment because, in addition to the organizational woes the system creates, there will be personal heartache in it, too. There is more to the story of what takes place when an administrator dares to fill one of those rarified positions, and it might rate as the tragicomedy of the era. Let us see what happens when . . . .

The Old Guard Meets the Fresh Blood

Holding a few top positions exempt from the constraints of civil service hiring is the way used by virtually all levels of government to allow elected officials to choose a limited number of their own lieutenants. Otherwise, there would be no way under heaven that they could hope to carry out any of their campaign promises. Elected officials must have a coterie of loyalists who share a determination to nail down at least a few of the planks in the election platform. The fabled failure of elected officials to live up to their campaign pledges may be more a function of the powerful resistence exerted by the civil servants inhabiting the systems they are "mandated" to change than their disgruntled constituents realize.

Every newly elected president of the United States is free to remove the previous president's top lieutenants and replace them with people considered more likely to carry out the new missions. The Congress must confirm certain critical choices to make sure the president, one fallible human being, makes no choices so poor as to jeopardize the welfare of the nation. An analogous situation holds at lower levels of government: the states, counties, and cities. Below this thin layer at the top they may not reach. Most terms of office are four years and, with some dramatic exceptions, two terms are expectable. What this means is that every four or eight years, the nation and an assortment of states, counties, and cities play fruit basket upset with their top management positions. The civil servants, who have weathered many changes of administration in the past, will weather many more while the bosses come and go in what seems an endless carnival dance. Nonetheless, when the new team comes in, they huddle and whisper about heads rolling, and fret incessantly about how top management changes will affect middle management and so on down the line. The work slows down and may virtually stop until these questions appear to be answered.

Newly elected officials are usually associated with either the fact or the myth of an electorate's desire for a change. Loath to ignore the people's mandate, change they do, or at least they try. To accompany the changes in top level personnel, there is often a flurry of reorganization activity within and among the diverse agencies under the governance of the newly elected. Thus, two of the questions of the civil servants are answered. Yes, middle management will be massively reassigned, and yes, the immediate superior one had grown used to will soon be somewhere else. The rumors about who will accede to the vacated position run rampant, and they are all of the dooms-day variety. No happy, wish-fulfillment rumors; they are consistently prepare-for-the-worst fantasies.

Just *try* managing an organization which is going through this kind of transformation. It doesn't help very much to know that you, and the changes you are insisting on implementing, are part of the problem. It is especially difficult when you are "the new kid on the block" and don't know any of the people, but they all know each other. Moreover, they have clearly defined you as the enemy. Every time your boss (the newly elected official) speaks at a press conference, you are in new trouble with your civil service subordinates. References to "a need for new ideas and approaches," "a time for change from old programs which aren't working," and "a need for an infusion of fresh blood" are, by their very nature, insulting to the old guard who consider themselves the targets of these remarks. This may or may not be correct. Often, the boss is taking a pot-shot at his or her predecessor's administration. Either way, it is the old guard who will be required to make and adjust to changes that are sure to be coming; and change is not the most popular activity known to humankind.

In time, if you are a good administrator, the organization may begin to work. You may feel sure that whatever it produces will soon be issuing forth copiously and well. This should occur in about August of the election year in which your boss either runs and loses or chooses not to run. Soon, you will be off to a new adventure, and the civil service regulars will be getting ready for the next administration. Should you return for a visit as much as six months later, you will find that the new administration and the regulars have rid the organization of all traces of your influence. You ruefully recall that you similarly enlisted the regulars' aid four or eight years earlier. The purging is especially clear-cut if the administration changes from conservative to liberal, or vice versa.

A favorite method chosen by new administrations for placing their imprimatur on an organization is to reorganize it. Thomas Backer, a psychologist who specializes in quality of worklife research, described the process in the following way.

> New administrations reorganize so as to create a tangible sense of territory. You make it your own by reorganizing, even if nothing much better will come out of it. I liken it to a dog lifting its leg to demarcate its territory. You get the message, but it's not a pleasant or productive one. And the result can do damage if the territory marked is a rug or a piece of furniture.

A particularly grandiose style of reorganization popular today is the consolidation of numerous small agencies into a single, sometimes immense, one. Chapter Three will describe some people who tend to promulgate this sort of thing. For example: "Empire Builders" do it for the obvious reason—to grab more territory. "Universe Tidiers" do it for less obvious reasons. It just seems tidier, somehow, to put all like functions together. Whatever the rationale, it often proves to be the undoing of the component parts. Therefore, the newly created whole will probably have to be dismantled, eventually. In government, it is usually by the succeeding administration. A selection of "war stories" will illustrate some of the critical sequelae of mergers, acquisitions, affiliations, or whatever label is applied, when two or more human service organizations were either forced to consolidate or tried, voluntarily, to unite for some mutually agreed upon purpose.

Merger Madness

It should be clear from the outset that when a very large organization and a very small organization unite, it may be referred to as a "merger" but it is, in fact, an "acquisition." The big organization acquires the little organization. Regardless of any euphemistically egalitarian rhetoric that may be used to persuade objectors, the big fish will eat the little fish and be influenced by the subtleties of its nature only briefly if at all. This was the situation when a former Secretary of Health and Welfare in one of the larger states attempted to carry out a "merger" of the Employment Department (ED) (12,000 plus employees) and the Department of Rehabilitation (DR) (2,000 plus employees). He was primarily a Universe Tidier; his empire did not promise to increase, it would simply become tidier. He reasoned that the Department of Rehabilitation was a highly specialized employment agency for disabled people and should not be fragmented from the larger employment operation. Also, he and his Governor looked forward to more "flexible" use of earmarked federal funds which the consolidation seemed to promise.

The plan was stopped by Senate testimony from an active consumer constituency which stated bluntly that the Department of Rehabilitation was a long way from good, but predicted it would become worse if buried within the gigantic Employment Department—stripped of direct access to the Secretary and the Governor, and deprived of protection from "flexible" uses of federal funds earmarked for the vocational rehabilitation of people with substantial disabilities. A small-scale experiment, to test the effects of consolidation at the local office level only, was the political face-saving substitute for the planned total merger. It turned out to be a useful experiment. After a three year test, the objections of the consumer constituency were confirmed. Although both agencies were, prima facie, concerned with employment (and were, in that sense, like functions), ED was basically a labor exchange which concentrated on offering employers needed workers to fill available jobs. DR, on the other hand, provided highly unusual services to would-be employees whose disabilities sharply limit their job choices. The two functions are very different, and require starkly divergent management styles. One of many possible illustrative examples will be offered. The entry level workers in the smaller Department had greater fiscal discretion (amount of money they could encumber without higher authorization) than middle managers approximately four rungs higher on the civil service ladder in the larger Department. Neither extreme reflected an error of policy-setting judgment. Each was appropriate to its own Department's functions and constraints, but they clashed formidably when put together. The Secretary was later reported to have acknowledged the error of his thinking, expressing relief that a "disaster" had been averted.

Unfortunately, there was no organized consumer constituency to avert his equally disastrous consolidation of five health-related agencies into a single, gigantic, Department of Health. Again, his empire did not expand, but it became conceptually tidier for him. Naturally, he expected to save the state money by eliminating duplications and distances. It didn't work. Described almost univocally as one of the state's worst managerial atrocities within the memory of observers, the lumbering giant floundered helplessly for five years before being redivided into five separate agencies.

A form of consolidation which is earnestly sought after by hospitals is "affiliation" with a medical school. The hospital stands to gain prestige, and all of the advantages that accrue to it, by becoming a "teaching hospital" for a medical school. More prestigious staff can be recruited, better funded research can be conducted, and the hospital staff have an opportunity to acquire university faculty status. The last is a personal boon, and also permits them to make longed-for inputs into training new generations of physicians and other health professionals. The university gains in having increased control over the settings in which medical education, research, and patient care take place.

The theory makes affiliation sound highly desirable for both parties. The practice, however, is often woefully disappointing and frustrating, especially for the hospital staff who have bartered some degree of autonomy for "advantages" appreciated abstractly if at all. Life at the university is relatively unchanged, except for the administrative annoyances of annexed hospital staff who resist handing over the reins. The experience of a large, well-established rehabilitation hospital in affiliating with a nearby medical school will serve to illustrate. The first blow for Hospital middle management was having a respected medical director driven out because his juggernaut style was intolerable to University powers—even though it had been highly effective in developing an internationally known patient care program. He was considered too headstrong to fit into the new milieu which was to be characterized by shared University/Hospital decision making.

The next blow was finding that he had been replaced by a person who never made any decisions at all. Practical, action-oriented department heads and medical service chiefs would stumble from his office in states of dull amazement after listening to lengthy philosophical discourses instead of the "yes" or "no" answers they had sought. They tried ganging up on him in twos, threes, and, finally, massive groups, but, singly or collectively, they failed ever to extract from him either a "yes" or a "no" with respect to some action to be taken.

The third blow was having prestigious University academician/clinicians deposited on top of them (organizationally speaking) to be superchiefs, as it were, who had the last word in spite of inexperience in running hospitals. Prestigious academician/clinicians are not necessarily the people you want making management decisions. (For more on this, see Chapter Three, "The Reblessed Professional and the Peter Principle.") Whether for good or ill, like the new Medical Director, for the most part, they didn't.

In a very few months, the changed priorities of the Hospital had become evident. First and second priorities went to "medical education" (primarily, training resident physicians in sundry specialty areas), and "medical research." "Patient care" appeared to be coming in a weak third. An ambience of gloom surrounded the patients as well as the staff, as the cumulative effects of absent leadership and conflicted management rose. It was not a wholesome environment for anyone. An exodus of staff, management and practitioner, began; and the reputation of the Hospital as one of the top half-dozen of its kind in the world plunged past zero to a negative image with larger and larger segments of the concerned community.

A change of medical directors, and a concerted effort to engage in reasonably nondefensive self-examination among key University and Hospital leaders, are reportedly bringing this Hospital back from the edge of disaster. Ironically, it may be too late. It now has to face the challenges of "Proposition 13," or "the California Taxpayers' revolt." If it survives this, together with the University, it may be able to rebuild its status as an outstanding patient care hospital. At least, as a free-standing facility, it will be relatively devoid of the next reorganization horror to be described. An important fulcrum, across which many politically controlled organizations swing, drunkenly, back and forth, is the issue of "centralization."

Centralization, Control, and Where the Action Is—And Isn't

Suppose an agency director who is opposed to the centralization of power has been in charge for several years and is then replaced by a procentralization leader.

In eight, or even four years' time, a great many functions can be decentralized. Decision-making authority can fan out to local offices, and their managers will be hustling busily to meet responsibilities and, perhaps, laying back occasionally to bask in the glow of their new-found power and importance. Support functions, such as equipment and space procurement, will be "outstationed" so the support staff will be knowledgeable about local needs and conditions. Therefore, they will be most useful and accessible to the scattered seats of power. Such decentralization is not easy to accomplish. Central office managers in charge of these functions will fight it every step of the way. They fear they will lose control of their subordinates to local managers who will co-opt them once they escape line-of-sight supervision. Difficult though it be, in four to eight years' time, a great deal of decentralization can be accomplished.

It is a pitiful sight to behold when a rather thoroughly decentralized organization is suddenly recentralized in a few months' time. It is as if a giant vacuum cleaner had been activated, that sucked all outcroppings of power back into the central office; not the people, just the power. Captivating rhetoric about the importance of having the entire team together for planning meetings pours forth abundantly to counter the concerns about having all of the decision makers so far from where the action is. After the power has been restored to the central office, there begins a more gradual process of retrieving the outstationed bodies, who are no longer needed by local managers because they are no longer responsible for the functions represented—or much of anything else. It is a forlorn time for the managers. "Yesterday I was a hero and today I'm a bum . . . Why?" is written on their faces as they shuffle aimlessly about, wondering what is left of their jobs. It is a hectic time for the support personnel; they must tell their families that it is time either to quit or to move. It is an anxious vacation for workers who are not directly affected, but sense the anger and depression around them. Consequently, they spend much of their time comparing rumors. Meanwhile, production, of whatever sort is intended for the organization, slips slowly off the bottom of the charts.

Centralization of power is a reasonable approach to take, and so is decentralization. Each has its own peculiar set of advantages and disadvantages, and which you prefer depends on which set you value more highly. What is unreasonable is whimsically switching back and forth from one to the other. Unfortunately, our system of allowing for exempt appointments, in the absence of any rules regarding what is permissible and nonpermissible with respect to reorganizations, encourages exactly this. "To centralize, or not to centralize" is a dilemma faced by every organization that boasts of more than one location. But there is an even pithier problem which arises when the organization delivers services that are regarded as a right or a privilege of the population. That issue has to do with "uniformity of services."

The Demand for Uniformity in a Nonuniform Universe

Government-operated human service agencies generally have what are referred to as "uniformity standards." That is, special or enriched services may not be offered to one part of the constituency unless they are available to all. In other words, if the ghetto doesn't get it, neither do the suburbs. Obviously, the favoritism to the rich at the expense of the poor implied by this comparison is exactly the kind of inequity such rules were contrived to avoid. When interpreted and applied, however, it often works the other way, too. If the suburbs don't get it, the ghetto can't have it either, unless it is clear that the suburbs don't need it at all. Such a schism between human needs in the ghetto and in the suburbs seldom exists. As a result, services needed more critically in one area than others may never be offered. It would be too costly to establish programs in every location with any degree of need.

In actual practice, high-level government decision makers have a great deal of latitude in the extent to which they stress or de-emphasize uniformity standards. When they choose to give emphasis, the accompanying rhetoric suggests they have no choice at all. The reason is this: in the process of applying the standards, some existing special programs are likely to be eliminated. In facing disgruntled constituents, and staff looking out for their interests, it is easiest to feign helplessness before a rule too stringent to confront. This is the old "my hands are tied" ploy.

The people who suffer most when an organization is placed in the charge of a "uniformity freak" (henceforward, UF), particularly if s/he is also "procentralization" (henceforward, PC), are the middle managers (henceforward, MMs). The PCUF will have little idea of what is going on at the local level—where the proverbial rubber hits the metaphorical road—either with staff or the people they serve. MMs may plead for license to conduct a special program which is wanted by their community, only to be parried with an answer that goes something like this: "You're being provincial to think that your clients are the only ones who need (blank). If you had the *big* picture, as we do in central office, you would know that *everyone's* clients need (blank). However, we don't have the funds to do it (territory) wide, and we can't do it anywhere until we do." MM goes home and tries to explain *that* to the local staff and the community, both of whom fail to understand why MM doesn't make decisions anymore. If they believe they're being "shucked" they get angry, and complain to the higher-ups about MM's changed responsiveness. That, of course, reaffirms the PCUF's decision to strip authority away from MMs, since they can't even handle community relations.

The "uniformity problem" is particularly vexing to forward-looking, future-oriented administrators because it strikes a lethal blow against state-of-the-art development of whatever helping art their agencies practice. Whether it delivers education, employment, health, welfare, or other social services, these innovative administrators want to see rapid state-of-the-art development so that today's "impossible cases" will become tomorrow's "piece o' cake." Much of the science supporting social/behavioral services does not go on in laboratories. It happens in real-world experiments and demonstrations testing approaches that someone thinks might work. Can you imagine a big bureaucracy implementing "an idea someone thinks might work" on a full-scale, territorywide basis? They won't. And if there are uniformity freaks at the helm of the organization, or running amok in a control agency, they won't let it happen in microcosm, either.

As a result, state-of-the-art advances in the human service fields must be left to the small, private, free-standing facilities, because they will not emerge from the big government-run bureaucracies. When each district office must conform to a regional office norm, and each regional office to a statewide norm, and, in programs with federal funding, each state must conform to a national norm—regardless of immense differences in need, available support resources, and environmental, economic, and other social conditions—a great leveling process is created which effectively prevents anything fresh, new, and, potentially, more workable from ever developing. The freedom to experiment, try new things on a small scale without going through the spontaneity-wrecking process of seeking grant funds which will not be subject to "audit exception" when used for a selected group, is essential if state-of-the-art improvements are to occur. The "research and demonstration" grant process is now the only path open to agency people who want to test new approaches. It usually doesn't work. On the rare occasions when a proposed project is blessed at all necessary levels, by the time the money comes through, the inspired individual who conceived of the project has long since given up and left for more rewarding employment. Those assigned to carry it out could usually care less. As a result, it fails. All concerned shake their heads about what a waste of time and money experimental projects are. And business goes on—as usual.

Chapter 3

Crazymakers: The People

Many administrators are able to adjust to the system without losing either their sanity or their integrity. Few, however, are prepared for some of the people they find inhabiting the system, or the interactions that may develop among them. Caught thus unprepared, they may alternately be reduced to states of frenzy, catatonia, or helpless merriment. For example, "Empire Builders" and "Survivors" are wrenchingly entertaining to observe. "Entertaining," for the obvious reason; they can be exceedingly funny. "Wrenchingly" so, because one sometimes catches a glimpse of oneself that one wasn't expecting to see.

This chapter deals with people such as these, and some fascinating combinations of people; for example, the mismated top management team comprised of a "revolutionary" and an old-line bureaucrat. The observations on which this chapter is based are drawn from a variety of public and private sector settings, and any resemblance to particular individuals, living, dead, or just burnt-out, is highly probable but nonetheless coincidental unless otherwise specified.

Empire Builders and Survivors

Pure "Empire Builders" want to expand and control as much as they possibly can. Pure "Survivors" are perfectly happy to stay where they are, the same size and shape, controlling about as much as they have grown accustomed to but not one whit less. Both come in all degrees of competence, relative to their work. There are a few "Combination" types, but they generally come to a bad end. It is an extremely stress-provoking combination of traits. "Empire building" always requires taking risks, and the "Survivor" does this grudgingly. Should a risk prove to have been a bad one, the suffering is unbearable.

The Empire Builder is an irritant to other Empire Builders, and irksome to Survivors who must stop the juggernaut from adversely affecting their plans for survival. They are vaguely amusing to most of the rest. On the other hand, the Survivor is a continual source of amazement to all. The incompetent-worker Survivor is an especially cherished source of "Can you believe this?" stories. For example, an outrageously incompetent fellow secured a high-level Washington position as a reward for diligent efforts during a political campaign. He managed to "land on his feet" (standard Survivor talk) in a powerless, but even more lucrative, civil service position when the new administration removed him, as one of their first official acts. Some speculate that one reason for his incompetence in the appointive position was that he spent full time on the matter of ensuring his subsequent survival. It worked, for him. However, the organization he headed substantially affected the expenditure of nearly one billion dollars per year. Therefore, his failure to function effectively was a continual source of frustration to many other administrators.

It should be noted that some people might be termed

"accidental empire builders." They are the creatively competent people who get so turned on to what they are doing that before they know it, an empire has developed. They are altogether different types of people and may belong in the "supersane" category. As such, they will be encountered again in the last chapter of the book. Only empire builders qua empire builders are the concern here.

Whereas Survivors always seem to come out smelling like the proverbial rose, Empire Builders frequently appear to be born for despair, especially those in the middle management ranks. First of all, despair is the lot of the insatiable. And to these individuals, the intervals between growth spurts are interminable and the joys of new acquisitions, orgastically brief. Moreover, they must continually worry that new top management directions will "reorg" their colonial holdings right out of existence. To prevent this, they may engage in an array of tactics—ranging from rather transparent, sycophantish manipulations to truly magnificent and complex Machiavellian strategems. Whether you are a colleague observing the process, or the unfortunate target of either the sycophant's obscene ministrations or the Machiavellian's thrusts, the result is the same. On good days, it's to laugh; on bad days, it's to sicken.

But these are only petty irritations which interfere with unabbreviated joy in going about one's administrative duties. It could be worse. One of the times when it *is* worse involves another pair of opposites. This pair is a team, a hideously mismated team, the top management team! They are . . . .

The Revolutionary and the Bureaucrat

The last two decades have seen a growing recognition that many citizens have been either intentionally or inadvertently stripped of their constitutional rights to: equal protection under the law, equal opportunity for education, equal employment opportunity, and, therefore, equal opportunity to earn a livelihood. At the same time, awareness has dawned that government agencies which deliver services to the minority, poor, or otherwise disenfranchised have been operating according to the belief, value, and knowledge systems of the predominant white middle class. Thus, both the services and their mode of delivery are planned and executed by people who are utterly unsophisticated about the realities and subtle nuances of the recipients' needs.

A first step toward correcting this was the establishment of "consumer advisory committees." The next was to augment affirmative action hiring efforts to ensure including some "consumer types" among new hirees and, also, promotees moving toward policy levels. A further step, for several sensitive-to-public-image elected officials, has been to appoint "consumer types" to top management positions, without concern for such preliminaries as significant work experience at less auspicious levels. To all appearances, this implicitly assumes that personal understanding of service users' needs is important qualifying background for top management positions and that administrative talent, skill, and experience are not. However, appearances deceive. In actual fact, the appointing power usually knows full well that the "indigenous leader" will be there only as a charisma-spreading symbol, to provide a unique brand of public relations, and not to run the agency. For that, the indigenous leader will be provided with backup, one or more experienced bureaucrats who can take care of business while the symbolic boss develops trust with the community, showing them how responsive the new-look government can be.

Elected officials inclined to appoint this type of figurehead are likely to be attracted to bright, young, energetic activists with revolutionary bents to their natures. The bureaucrats selected to be the power-behind-the-throne are also apt to be bright, but could never be considered revolutionary spirits. If they were, they would have been long gone from the scene where the drama is unfolding. This unlikely team may get along well, in the beginning. The revolutionary knows the appointment was contingent on accepting some such arrangement. The bureaucrats know that this is the closest they will ever come to holding a "number one" position.

In one interesting case, a middle-aged bureaucrat seeking

to regain his lost youth was so assigned. The honeymoon lasted a bit longer than expected because he found the revolutionary a fascinating, youthful spirit with whom to identify. But revolutionaries and longtime bureaucrats are very different types of people, and the honeymoon did, eventually, end. The two ultimately discovered that beneath their facades of mutual respect for nonoverlapping, complementary capabilities lay intensely conflicting values, goals, and styles. Each battled constantly to prevent the other from bringing down what was seen as sure ruination upon them both. The bureaucrat convinced the revolutionary, naive in such matters, that certain protocols had to be followed lest all revolutionary goals be forfeited forever. This was a ruse, of course. The need resided solely in the bureaucrat who, over the years, had developed a strong sense of what constitutes organizational tidiness. The protocols related to commonplace rules, designed to be bent by whomever would bend them. Uniformity of services, discussed earlier, illustrates the type of issue involved.

On the other hand, the revolutionary convinced the bureaucrat that the consumer community would declare war if ways were not found to accomplish certain ends. This, too, was not true. It was primarily the revolutionary who wanted them to happen; as many consumers opposed as favored the approaches. When the bureaucrat obediently found ways, many consumers were angry and began to make trouble.

Most difficult of all, the revolutionary had never attended a four-day wonder course and was not in command of the "management truth" that a new top executive must play "the new kid on the block," observing but passing no judgments, for a decent interval after assuming the job. Then, modest changes (which are not inherently insulting to the old guard) may be tossed out for participative consideration. Instead, the revolutionary flamingly denounced the extant operation, promising the media that, "Things will change or heads will roll!" He thence attempted to transform the agency into his preconceived, ideal image overnight. In the ensuing chaos, polarizing forces developed and efforts were made to shift the blame of attributed failures from one cluster of shoulders to another. As news of groundswells of rebellion among the workers in field offices reached central office, directives began to be issued and countermanded, decisions were made and rescinded, as various forces struggled to claim control over the top team. By this time it was highly vulnerable to such efforts, due to its lack of unity and its desperate need for support coming from somewhere.

The revolutionary and the bureaucrat blamed each other for their fiascos and blunders. Number One gradually became more public about it; Number Two chose to unburden by lamenting Number One's ineptitude to the next level of lieutenants. Since both were bright, each, eventually, caught on to what the other was doing. It took a long time to resolve the problem. The revolutionary was considered a political liability to the elected official ("You can't get by with placing a non-administrator in a highly visible administrative job forever"), so Number One was reluctant to "make waves." The bureaucrat knew that when it ended the chances for a worse assignment exceeded those for a better one. Thus, Number Two did not want to "make waves" either. When it finally became unbearable, they agreed to dissolve the team.

It can be viewed as a noble experiment which failed. The idea of appointing a symbolic leader, who truly understands and inspires the trust of service recipients, and teaming that person with an experienced, capable, strong administrator who, first, is a good manager of people and, second, adheres to the maxim, "Tell the boss what you really think and don't give a damn whether you have a job tomorrow," has potential merit. In practice, however, the revolutionaries have too often been chosen emotionally and carelessly, the bureaucrats have been picked adventitiously, and the teams have not been selected *as teams:* screened, in part, by examining how honestly and effectively they can work together.

The revolutionary and the bureaucrat are a fascinating pair to watch, but there is another pairing which is equally intriguing and far less painful to observe because their conflict is less deadly for the organization. There will be lots of fireworks and good, clean fun when you have . . .

Two Charismatic Leaders in the Same Organization

If one of them supported the other, perhaps there would be no problem, but charismatic leaders tend not to surround themselves with other leaders, charismatic or otherwise. They tend, in fact, to surround themselves with pliable drones who will radiate no distracting light of their own to confuse the superstar's issues and strategems, and who can be counted on to support his or her preferences. Thus, one does not expect to see Peter, Paul, and Mary sharing the limelight and filling in for one another. One may expect to see the gingham dog and the calico cat engaged in a battle of about the cosmic significance suggested by those antagonists. It happens any time and anywhere that two charismatic leaders are thrust upon one another if both are devoted to the same mission. However, it is particularly comical to watch in a human service agency where each of the superstars believes s/he is "The Savior" of the downtrodden souls whom the agency serves.

A story will illustrate what can happen. Once upon a time, and it was not so very long ago, a rather plain, but solid, administrator hired a superstar-savior to run a program designed to help dissatisfied clients seek redress from the system. With some misgivings but with great, high hopes, he instructed his new "chief ombudsman" to act in good conscience. Then, he stayed out of his way, to avoid any charges of trying to co-opt the critic. The ombudsman was still in place when the plain, but solid, administrator was replaced by, you guessed it, another messiah! Similar in nature to the "revolutionary" just described, this one saw no earthly reason why the flock he meant to save required additional saving by another. Although he had succeeded admirably in ridding the organization of others he saw as unfit or superfluous, he utterly failed in herculean efforts to dispense with the ombudsman, who had the ear of someone outranking his messianic superior in the larger administrative hierarchy.

For months the battle raged, each proclaiming he would

save (various) factions of the consumer constituency from the full range of evils that befall humankind and, with their support, from the other "savior" as well. It finally ended over a contractual technicality. But it was fun while it lasted, for everyone except the layers of administrators caught in between. They had nonvoluntarily provided the conduits through which communications between the two ebbed and flowed. This used up a great deal of time during the "engagement," and they, consequently, had a great deal of catching up to do when it was over. Moreover, they were plain tired.

Ironically, these two charismatic leaders should have found a certain solace and friendship in each other. They had more in common than being saviors. They were also two of the rare individuals in the entire organization who were not, and had never been, professional human service workers. Most of the administrators in human service agencies are "reblessed professionals" who have been promoted out of their fields and into the field of administration, without benefit of vocational guidance. But herein lies another tale.

The Reblessed Professional and the Peter Principle

To begin this section, here is a definition of "the Peter Principle." In essence, it states that, "In an organization, one rises to one's level of incompetence and there one stays!" (Peter, 1969). Please keep this in the back of your mind as you read on.

It is surely safe to say that the majority of administrators in human service fields did not start out to be administrators. They did not major in public or business administration when they went to college, and, for the most part, they never planned, hoped, or even thought about being administrators one day. A significant number of them planned, hoped, and thought about becoming doctors, psychologists, nurses, social workers, rehabilitation counselors, occupational therapists, and other varieties of people helpers too numerous to mention. It can be assumed that, like other people, they had dreams of glory that included advancement in their careers. If they were not destined to join the world's renowned in their fields, just being a member of one of those lofty professions seemed satisfying and prestigious enough. Or so they thought when they began.

If they went to work in a big bureaucracy, they soon learned that the only road to glory required something other than advancing within the field. It required leaving it, for the new field of administration. The first step toward abandoning their planned careers and taking on an adventitious one happened with the promotion to supervisor, whether it was called "supervisor," "chief of staff," or some other equivalent title. A sizable chunk of their work time began draining into matters managerial, accompanied by vague feelings of having lost touch with *the people*, whether clients, patients, students, or otherwise designated service consumers. But power feels good, even to people helpers, and before very long, these troublesome feelings of discontent are put away and the person starts scaling the ladder, leaving direct services farther and farther behind to other people, the cream of which crop will one day begin the same journey.

Although they are the cream of the professional crop, they may not prove to be the cream of administrators. In fact, the very traits, personality and otherwise, that render them visibly successful in their professional fields may militate against their being outstanding administrators. However, since the competitors for administrative jobs have been similarly selected, and there are few administratively trained candidates with whom to compare them, full awareness of their deficiencies is lacking. Some degree of awareness is present, however. This is witnessed by the fact that brand-new reblessed professionals-turned-administrators are bustled off to a dizzying variety of four-day wonder courses in the theory, principles, and practices of management. Sometimes it "takes" and sometimes it doesn't. There are reasons of temperament which lead certain people to select careers as administrators and lead others to choose careers as people helpers. Those differences will not be crushed under the weight of a thousand four-day wonder courses.

Once again, a true story provides an example. A remarkably capable counselor tried to manage a halfway house where rule infractions and behavioral disturbances were the order of the day. Being a counselor, he dealt with such occurrences as if they were counseling problems. They were, however, administrative issues, and there is an important difference if mayhem and anarchy are to be avoided. In the halfway house situation, if one is sensitive enough to sniff out a problem before it results in a rule infraction, then it is a counseling problem. One counsels the person in an effort to "head off" the infraction, prevent the disturbance from occurring. However, failing in this, once it has happened, the problem is administrative and there are sanctions to be applied. This need not foreclose on counseling with the person *later*, to aid in dealing with the pain and teachings of punitive or corrective sanctions. One does not, however, counsel *instead*.

Unfortunately, many people helper administrators do. They empathize all too well with the inner pressures and histories of painful experience that lead one to clobber a roommate or break other rules. As a result, it is very difficult for this type of administrator to "blindly follow the book," or "rigidly adhere to dehumanizing procedures"—which is how the counselor-administrator of this story saw the rules he was purportedly there to enforce. By substituting "psychotherapy" for punitive/corrective sanctions, he avoided the anxiety of appearing unhelpful and being labeled a "bad guy" by one of the residents. The latter, in turn, figured out that the worst you can get for the worst you can do is a nice little talk with the boss.

The anxiety aroused by the prospect of appearing to be a "bad guy" may be the deadliest killer of effective administrators that exists. Although it is not unique to them, it is a disease to which people helpers easily fall prey. Most difficult, the ethics of their occupational subculture forces them to lie about it to themselves. They risk being labeled "neurotic" and "unfit" if they publicly acknowledge that they are nurtured and gratified by appreciation and love from their helpees. Although freedom from such needs may be theoretically ideal, realistically speaking, it is not always found. Many people helpers, if permitted to be honest on the subject, enter the field, at least in part, because they want and need those "strokes." They love it when they receive them, and they are sorely distressed when they don't.

This personality trait does not disappear the day they get promoted to supervisor. The source of their sustenance is simply transferred from helpees to subordinates. Under circumstances such as these, how many critical performance evaluations do you suppose they write? The answer is, "Not very many." Lamentably, employees doing less than acceptable work might profit greatly from receiving accurate feedback about their deficiencies early enough in their careers to do something about them. But a great many supervisors find such confrontation overly difficult, even when it would be in the best interest of their subordinates.

If it is difficult for the administrator to forfeit the goodwill of one person, imagine what having to make one of those renowned moves known as "unpopular administrative decisions" could do. These, by definition, lose the decision maker the love and forbearance of from fifty to one hundred percent of the organization. In this perverse world, however, it seems that many of the best administrative decisions are unpopular, at least at first. This is because they usually entail a degree of change that is unnerving until familiarity takes root. Administrators who are especially vulnerable to the slings and arrows that follow such action avoid it, often by attempting to manage "by consensus."

The problem is, consensus is unattainable. When everyone is asked, and not everyone can be satisfied, more than affection may be lost. Tempers go, too, and in ways the hapless administrator is unprepared for. In the face of rebellion, unpopular decisions, including good ones, may be rescinded before having a chance to demonstrate their workability. The approval-driven administrator loses credibility, and the organization is well on its way to becoming a proof of the second law of thermodynamics. This, you will recall, states, roughly, that a closed system tends to run down, or move from a state of differentiation to one of undifferentiated chaos. At this point, one could reasonably claim that the administrator in question had come face to face with that other law of the social universe which was defined at the beginning of this section, the Peter Principle.

In looking at human service administrators and the stock from which they come, it is important to remember that not all people helpers are People Helpers. Actually, People Helpers are only one of three basic personality types which inhabit human service organizations. The three have little in common beyond each taking a fierce pride in being totally incapable of understanding the other two. The three types are . . .

People Helpers, Crass Materialists, and Universe Tidiers

"People Helpers" are people who are motivated to help (remold) other people. They like to help others solve their problems and correct their deficiencies in order to watch them go forth, happy and productive. As discussed earlier, their rewards come partly in the form of gratitude, appreciation, and love from those whom they help, although they tend to deny this. They also tend to deny all but a minimal interest in money. Actually, it is hard to get them to admit what they are getting out of it, but there must be something.

"Crass Materialists" not only do not deny but gleefully proclaim an all-abiding interest in money, much to the discomfiture of the People Helpers. Some choose the more lucrative helping professions for this reason, and others seek ever higher promotions. A few, of course, do both. They appear to feel no sense of shame while parking their Lincolns next to the People Helpers' Fords.

"Universe Tidiers," as a group, are somewhat enigmatic. They have no great, altruistic desire to minister unto others, nor have they overweening desires for material goods. They simply like—no, they *need*—to make everything tidy. A sense of maldistributed goods gives them the bends. Pain, like poverty, disturbs them because it seems messy, somehow. Although they are not particularly compassionate or generous people, seeing suffering distresses them—like pictures hanging crooked on a wall. Only to this third group is the reward in the doing. The relief that comes from tidying yet another messy little corner of the universe is truly ecstatic for the pure Universe Tidier personality. They don't have to wait until someone says, "thank you" or pays them to feel good. They rather feel sorry for the Materialists, with whom they are seldom confused, for being reliant on unreliable external rewards. They regard People Helpers, with whom they are frequently confounded, as self-deluding. Nonetheless, they sometimes "pass" as People Helpers simply because it is so much easier to explain.

The three personality types are so utterly alien to one another that they may as well have come from different planets. They continually misinterpret each others' motivations, assuming them to be akin to their own. What one regards as a solution is to another, a problem. Communication is practically impossible, and managing an organization of noncommunicating aliens is no easy matter. The People Helpers and the Crass Materialists are apt to file grievances against one another on a variety of work-related pretexts, but, au fond, what they are grieving is each other's existence. Universe Tidiers find grievances messy. Consequently, they leave them on their desks past the deadline for responding, causing grievances to be filed against *them.*

As if all this didn't make things complicated enough for the administrator, the people in the organization will be divided in yet another troublesome way. Specifically . . .

Men, Women, and the Good Old Boys

In noticeable numbers, women are newcomers to the administrative echelons of work organizations, and the two sexes understand each other there about as well as anywhere else. Other writings have pointed out that women appear not to have learned how to "play the game" with the good old boys. One example related this to a lack of childhood experience—specifically, learning that they even need kids they hate on their football teams. However, the reactions of white,

male administrators to minority male newcomers is often similar. As with women, there are highly visible physical differences,
and there are also subcultural differences of behavior—dress,
idiom, situational response patterns, and other aspects of being.
These render "us-them" distinctions easy to make and hard to
forget. Differences of any kind are apt to be unwelcome because they threaten change. However, the differences presented
by women and minorities are particularly resisted because both
are traditional social underdogs. Underdogs are not readily relin-
quished by upperdogs who wish to maximize the space between
themselves and the bottom. One way to punish or discourage
such intruders is to deny them access to needed communication
channels; and the good-old-boy network is often the only reasonably effective way for getting things done. This creates genuine problems for women and minority men who take on key
administrative roles that can in no way be attributed to differences in their early childhood experiences.

Both women and minority men run the risk of being
placed in token or figurehead positions, these days. Sometimes
they understand this beforehand, and sometimes they discover
it only after painful, personal lessons about political realities.
The organization may suffer, too, if they insist upon trying to
do a real job where none was meant to exist—and does not, in
the minds of those whose cooperation is needed.

Sometimes the particular woman (or minority man) involved is the biggest part of the problem. Exaggerated zeal for
affirmative action is elevating women and minority men to positions which exceed their competency with increasing frequency.
This creates unique coping problems for the people who are
"over their heads" because admitting incompetence or failure is
far more than a personal issue. They may believe, and sometimes correctly so, that such an admission will do social harm to
the entire group they "represent." Thus, they may hang on
tenaciously, becoming increasingly defensive as their fears of
public disgrace and political regression for their "constituen-
cies" mount. At the same time, whoever appointed them will be
much more fearful of removing them than would be true with a
nonsymbolic appointee. The coping problems for people around

them will be little different from those of dealing with any other subcompetent superior or colleague, but may be experienced more intensely.

Also "experienced more intensely" is the human reaction to women in authority. Researchers at the University of Dayton found that people of both sexes were more critical of a woman employer who punished a male subordinate than they were of a male employer who meted out equivalent punishment to a male subordinate. They were also more critical of a woman employer who was lenient with a female subordinate than they were of a male employer who was equivalently lenient. Even given that such a perceptual/judgmental bias exists, many thinkers on the subject still maintain that some women administrators believe they must sacrifice their femininity in order to become effective. The same psychologist who so provocatively likened the reorganization urge to canine territory marking has designated this "the mail order balls syndrome." Some women administrators may impair their potential competence by charading as "the meanest sonofabitch in the valley" or some other defeminized image, and fail to put their fresh and valuable perspectives and approaches to good use. An analogous situation has been observed among ethnic minority people who become "whiter than white," losing the valuable differences which their backgrounds afford them. Perhaps nowhere are new and different ways of perceiving and solving problems more critically needed than in the field of administration. Their loss, because women and minority administrators feel constrained to adopt the ways of the dominant culture, is tragic. The struggle to maintain one's differences, while trying to "fit in" to an established system of values and protocols, is a formidable one. It seems clearly worth the effort for those who are able, but the pitfalls are many, and some are insidiously subtle.

An intriguing research report revealed that men who claimed to be in favor of women's liberation showed *less* affection for career women than avowed male chauvinists. Au contraire, they showed more affection for women described as homemakers than did the avowed chauvinists. One could speculate endlessly about this seeming paradox, or continue, as

e. e. cummings might put it, "To prod their inner versus outer worlds with the naughty thumb of science." Whatever course chosen, and whatever the reasons for the discrepancies of attitude among "liberal" males, the differences in men's and women's management styles are readily apparent and no one is leeringly proclaiming, "Vive la difference!"

If you are one of the good old boys and the smoke-filled rooms are suddenly inhabited by a mixed-sex group, the change can be traumatic. Some of the newcomers, whom you are inclined to call "chicks" but are enjoined to call "women," are young enough to be your daughter. It was unsettling enough when your new, immediate superior turned out to be contemporary with your son, but that you were somewhat prepared for. What man doesn't know, in his heart, that one day the young turks will take over, and he will be on the way out? But whoever thought that some of the young turks would be *girls*? You begin to question the meaning of your entire working life. What has it meant, to come to this? What do you tell your wife, so that she'll continue to take your work seriously? How do you introduce them at the Christmas party? How do you explain that *that* little snippet is "the old man"?

If you're her, the trauma is leavened with the excitement of a bold, new adventure, but it is trauma, nonetheless. The hostility around you brings on chilly nights in the middle of blistering days. You are numbly aware that you have achieved a longtime ambition; you are in a room filled with men and not one of them has designs on your body (except, maybe, to kill it). Depending on your own nature and temperament, you are destined to become either a subservient, a militant, or, with a little bit of luck, a person who will just do your own thing and rise above it. Any reaction but the last is sure to raise hell in the organization; and even the last can't prevent the turmoil that will probably arise anyway.

On the subject of differences, a woman who breaks down and cries during a heated discussion is construed as the irrefutable proof that women are out of place in such settings; not only by the men, but by any other women present as well. The women will quickly reformulate their conclusions to read, "This *particular* woman is out of her element and should acknowledge that fact." But for an instant, the denigrating programming regarding "women's ways," and, especially, untrammeled emotional expression, will burst forth from even the women. They will be embarrassed and angered by such an atavistic regression that could threaten the administrative viability of them all.

It is really too bad. There is nothing more inherently disruptive about crying than the angry blustering which men sometimes do to relieve similar frustrations—and which is found perfectly acceptable. In fact, crying is probably less destructive to goal-directed behavior because it is honest and direct. It relieves frustrations and is obviously what it is. The masculine style of pseudological ramrodding is often nothing but disguised crying which diverts the negotiations far from their intended course. Sometimes this is never discovered, or if it is, no one knows how it happened, or when, or why. As women's styles of managing and being become more familiar in administrative circles, their different, but perfectly natural, behaviors will become more acceptable, too. In this time of transition, the men may "discover" some of them as alternatives that generate fewer secondary problems.

This brings us to the end of the conditions to be described which contribute substantially to the burning out of administrators. The whole range of crazymaking situations one stumbles into, coupled with a rapidly dwindling reservoir of rewards to make it all worthwhile, can reasonably be defined as *hell*. Hell, it turns out, is both "other people" and "the system." It lacks brimstone, but it does get hot—and the predictable conflagrations occur. In the process, untold numbers of administrators get severely burnt out. The next chapter looks at the consequences of bearing the massive pressures described in the first three chapters.

Chapter 4

The Result

Given the multitudes of crazymaking possibilities and the infinite combinations and permutations in which they can occur, it is unlikely that the same situation will ever befall two administrators. Even if it did, it is even more unlikely that they would respond in the same way. Therefore, this chapter will present a conceptual montage of an array of survival gyrations which have been observed, along with selected images of what happens to the behavioral styles of administrators as they give up the struggle. There are tell tale signs to look for, in oneself and one's compatriots, if one is to recognize what is occurring in time to halt and reverse the process.

Administrator as Juggler

Professional jugglers have to be able to keep three balls in the air for a matter of minutes in order to win the applause of the crowd. Administrators must practice such legerdemain on dozens of "balls," sometimes interminably, with no expectation that anyone will clap or even mumble, "Well done." The "balls", in this case, are the demands, pressures, constraints, double binds, mixed messages, and dysfunctional policies, procedures, and practices described in the first three chapters, plus both real and illusory opportunities that sing their siren songs from the rocky shores.

To gain a broader perspective on the sum total effect as these forces conjointly impinge on some unsuspecting executive in the human service industry, the author spoke with dozens of administrators about what a typical day, or a typical week, was like for them. Most of them sounded like Mack Sennet interpretations of Greek tragedies. During the recountings, the author's visual imagery took on the fast-motion, jerky quality of early silent cinema. This proved highly appropriate to the story lines of slapstick comedies of errors with actors charging off in wrong directions, as well as for the frequent melodramas of hopeless exasperation. Few related any contact whatsoever with the people their agencies serve, but an exception came from the Personnel Director of a large sheltered industry (a work setting that hires a high percentage of workers with physical/mental disabilities and allows some degree of failure to meet ordinary production standards).

Because he was in the process of preparing for an accreditation site visit, he was acutely aware of the vexing nature of having to repeatedly shift mental set from one appropriate for expansive, future-oriented, long-term planning, to one suitable for here and now "administrivia" (a coined word meaning just what it appears to: administrative trivia). The two functions require very different kinds of consciousness which develop momentum with use, and the momentum is lost each time a shift must be made. Added to this was his frustration in knowing that many of the problems encountered arose from the failure of higher levels of management to initiate preparations much earlier. It was becoming depressingly clear that certain shortcomings could not be corrected in time. Moreover, other division heads were less responsive to his requests for information and materials than they would have been to a superior; and higher-ranking individuals had always been in charge of this activity before.

Meanwhile, the other duties of a personnel director would not wait; people still had to be hired, processed, and fired. Although firings are accompanied by careful documentation to avoid grievances, our juggler was nonetheless pulled away from accreditation preparations time after time to attend hearings and, on one occasion, to appear in court. While he scurried from stage right to stage left, a new ball came toward him from stage front. A consumer organization was demanding that all workers in sheltered industries be paid at least minimum wage, regardless of whether their production approximated standard, simply because they were human beings who deserve a living wage. As he settled into his chair to formulate a position on this issue, an employee who had been fired for being drunk on the job came in, again drunk, demanding reinstatement lest he file a complaint with the Fair Employment Practices Commission.

When closing time came, the Personnel Director determined to come in for a few hours on the weekend to work on accreditation preparations when there would be no interfering distractions. As he left the building, he said, "goodnight" to a worker named Brian, and recalled when he had first come to know him. It was three years earlier, during the previous period of preparing for an accreditation site visit. Brian's lack of attention to personal hygiene had become seriously obtrusive during the summer months, but he had not responded to suggestions, then to pleas, requests, and finally demands that he shower more often. His supervisor decided it was a personnel matter and referred him to you-know-whom for a little Dutch Uncle counseling. It turned out that tutoring, not counseling, was needed. Their meeting evolved into a demonstration, in the facility adjacent to the nurse's office, of the subtleties of taking an effective shower. Brian was rather severely mentally retarded and had emulated television commercial actors rubbing their bodies all over with soap, without realizing that they wet and lathered it first. The Personnel Director noted idly that Brian's hygiene seemed quite acceptable now. With that thought, he smiled a little and the spring came back into his walk.

This administrator denies that he is now, ever has been, or ever will be burnt out. He says he does this type of work as a substitute for the priesthood, a childhood goal and family expectation he gave up when he discovered girls in his junior year of high school. His decision to subject himself to a frenzying pace which often culminates in disappointments fits into a rather well-thought-out philosophy of life and purpose, leaving very little dissonance to be resolved. Besides, Brian was not an isolated case. The Personnel Director has many opportunities to give direct help to people in need, despite his organizational status. This makes the rest worthwhile.

Most administrators no longer have, or make, such opportunities. Perhaps if they did, it would provide the leavening needed to lighten their administrative burdens. It is almost impossible, however, for administrators who rise to central office positions in large agencies where all services take place in geographically remote field offices. A former Assistant Director in a large bureaucracy of this type described the juggling act she performed for months, with no such leavening, and under extremely difficult circumstances.

She was appointed by a new, "liberal" male Director who believed he should appoint at least one woman to a high post. She struck him as a little "square," but he felt he had no other choices. Her reputation was one of competence and integrity, and she was the highest ranking woman in the agency. She was, however, naive. When he told her he wanted honest feedback on his ideas, she believed him and gave it. The good old boys made no such mistakes. By contrast, her criticisms were seen as evidence that she could not "tune in" to the new ways of doing things. Therefore, she was never delegated the full authority that ordinarily accompanied the post. To avoid hurting her feelings (since she was a woman), she was not told this directly. Instead, she found it out little by little, each time her boss pulled the rug out from under her. With the chorus chanting, "No support from above" offstage, she began her daily prestidigitation.

One week's calendar showed meetings covering the following range of topics: long-range planning, short-range planning, program evaluation criteria, worker performance standards, special services of three different types, civil rights issues, legislative problems, services to bilingual clients, conflict of interest issues, zero-based budgeting, liaison with other community agencies, an experimental project, and a meet-and-confer with the union bargaining team. This required her, within a one-week period, to think like: a futurist, a lawyer, a statistician, a scientist, a human service practitioner, a personnel analyst, an accountant, a politician, a sociologist, a public realtions expert, a diplomat, and, incidentally, an administrator. She worked approximately eleven and one-half hours each day in order to stay "afloat."

Following up on the meet-and-confer a few days later, she flew to the field office that was the site of the union-stimulated unrest. She presented her decision on the matter, one formulated expressly to be fair to both the union and middle management. She regretted that there was no time to see a little of the action with clients while she was there. Afterward, as she arrived at the airport, she received an emergency call from a member of her central office staff. The Director, whose sympathies were known to be with the union far more than with middle management, had already reversed her decision.

She was relieved of her post a few months later and replaced by a good old boy who fit very well into the now all-male team. From what he tells her, most of the problems she foresaw and tried to avoid have come to pass. She, meanwhile, took nearly two years to recover from a severe case of burn out. She has now taken a comparable position in a smaller agency. She "screened" her prospective superior very carefully this time. She says she enjoys juggling when the balls are not tethered by invisible wires under someone else's control.

Many others, however, do not enjoy it at all. Those who do often find the balls compelled by forces other than their own and that of gravity, and no degree of skill can render their trajectories predictable. It is, perhaps, this absence of predictability which is the major cause of burn out. Animal studies dating from the fifties (Richter, 1957) have demonstrated that loss of contact with information channels needed for survival and consequent loss of control over survival-related outcomes can lead to behaviors suggesting hopelessness, giving up, and, finally, even death. Observations of primitive peoples, surgery patients, college sophomores, and others have shown that severed ties, actual or imagined, between action and outcome may provoke similar reactions in humans. In short, we may grasp at straws as long as there are any in sight, but when the last one disappears, a sense of futility combines with fatigue in a way that defeats further effort.

The Last Struggle

The prodromal stages of impending burn out often take the form of exaggerated effort within a constricted band of activities or concerns. Just as the pupillary reflex is to constrict and sharpen focus under stress, the larger behavioral script is similarly characterized. Among administrators, this may be illustrated by referring to a tool familiar to many: the *Styles of Leadership Survey* (Hall and Williams, 1968). In it, five basic styles of leadership are described in terms of the administrator's concerns for the goals and tasks of the organization, and the people in it. The person who shows high concern for both is said to use a "Team Management" (people support what they help create) style. This is the most effective alternative. If a more moderate, but still balanced, degree of concern for both is shown, this is a "Middle of the Road Management" (be firm but fair) style, and is next best to the ideal. The unbalanced styles are problematical. High concern for goals, coupled with low concern for people, generates a "Task Management" (produce or perish) style, and the reverse creates a "Country Club Management" (try to win friends and influence people) style. Low concern for either is designated "Impoverished Management" (don't rock the boat) style and has no redeeming virtues.

Many administrators can function as Team Managers or, at least, Middle of the Road Managers under favorable conditions. They are able to see that production results from an integration of task and human requirements. They believe that both good relationships and high production are attainable, and see their responsibilities as achieving effective production through participation and involvement of people and their ideas. At the very least, a middle ground of reasonable production and decent morale will be sought.

Under pressure, however, they are apt to slip into one of the unbalanced styles. Which one depends largely on temperament and partly on circumstance. Some may narrow their vistas and focus overmuch on tasks, relegating good relationships to a poor second place. They are also apt to take over more of the planning, directing, and controlling. This usually proves unsuccessful, as the law of reverse effort (see Chapter Two) would predict. Others may manifest their sense of being overwhelmed by uncontrollable forces through focusing excessively on the people, placing production incidental to harmonious relationships. The task is too much; they just want everyone, themselves included, to be happy.

Such coping strategies are not necessarily pathological adjustments, in the short run. They happen naturally, and to the best of administrators. However, when an administrator who has been capable of balanced management in the past finds that s/he is operating in one of the unbalanced styles over a prolonged period of time, it would be wise to inquire of one's inner self if this is indicative of a latent chronic state. Does it reflect an attempt to fend off too much stimulation from too many divergent, unpleasantly surprising sources by narrowing the field of involvement and pouring one's excessive nervous energy into an ever shrinking aperture? In other words, ask whether it signifies a prodromal stage of burn out.

"Last struggle" behavior often reflects a quality of impaired judgment that may appear as the activation level of the individual declines. An example concerns an administrator in an agency under seige from a newly formed professional workers' union. Have you ever seen labor and management sitting on the same side of the bargaining table? This administrator found the emerging rift between the two groups, both of which he defined as "good guys," so intolerable that he literally refused to acknowledge the reality of what was happening. He treated meet-and-confer sessions as if they were soireés, and he, an intellectual gadfly, speaking now for management, now for labor. The naive observer might have mistaken his behavior for egalitarianism. That would be naive, indeed. Psychologists have a better phrase for it: "identification with the aggressor." One identifies with the aggressor in hopes of being spared. When the czars sense that the bolsheviks are on their way to becoming the new czars, they are apt to smile and nod a great deal.

A fascinating theory which may reflect a reciprocating cause and effect of burn out in the upper echelons has been developed by a researcher concerned with cardiovascular disease (Kemp, 1977). It is addiction to one's own biochemistry—specifically, a high level of adrenalin production. As with central nervous system stimulants which are taken by mouth or injected into the bloodstream, there appears to be a need for increasing "dosages" of internally produced adrenalin for equivalent effect. Since the means for increasing the dose is behavioral, adrenalin-producing behavior is increasingly evinced. Enjoinders to "slow down and relax," which occur as the signs of strain become evident to others, may be consciously accepted. Unconsciously, however, they are resisted because the entreated behavioral change would result in withdrawal symptoms of let down and depression rather than an improved state of being. In a similar vein, Hans Selye, the Canadian physiologist famous for his research and theories on the causes and effects of stress, points out that some people are "racehorses" while others are "turtles," both quite naturally. He asserts that trying to force a racehorse to slow down may be as stressful as trying to force a turtle to hurry. Some of the apparent "racehorses" may be adrenalin addicts, however, who might be happier if they could find their way back a little closer to turtledom.

If it is true that some people become addicted to high adrenalin output which their lifestyles have engendered, it is probably also true that some of the afflicted are those ambitious, achievement-oriented souls who become administrators. This could be troublesome enough for the individual concerned, but it is pure hell for associates. The reason is, a good way to ensure a steady supply of the "drug" would be to engage continually in that high-risk behavior known as "brinksmanship." An administrator known to the author appears to fit such a pattern very well, and will be used to illustrate how the addiction could be both a cause and an effect of the burning-out process.

This individual worked as a public administrator for many

years before coming face to face with the realization that there is more to life than he had sampled. Rather suddenly, he wanted desperately to diversify before it was too late. Unable to break free from the security trap (see Chapter Two) which he had built for himself over the years, he vascillated uncomfortably between semileaving and semistaying, sharing his conflict with anyone who would listen. The spectre of the "Impoverished Manager" haunted him, and he fought quixotically against it. He discovered that he could keep his rebelling spirit in line by throwing everything he had into whatever problem adventitiously arose. His conflict between competing desires to maintain his security versus starting anew was reflected in a management style wherein he ricocheted dizzyingly back and forth between the two unbalanced styles of management. One moment, harmony among colleagues was all that really mattered. In the next, he might react wildly to a long-predicted downturn in production which neither alarmed nor even surprised anyone else. He developed a pattern of overreacting to minor incidents, and escalating them to crisis proportions. And it sometimes seemed that, underneath the facade of agitation and annoyance, he thrived on the helter-skelter that ensued. His subordinates longed for a little of the benign neglect attributed to the "Impoverished Manager." Considering everything, it seems reasonable to speculate that this man had grown addicted to a high level of adrenalin in his system.

One might expect that adrenalin addiction would be accompanied by some degree of addiction to alcohol, since some way must be found to "come down." The individual described frequently drank to excess and saw this as a significant problem in his life. Being imbued with the culturally dominant psychogenic theories of the etiology of alcoholism, it never occurred to him to relate his blitz drinking urges to a physiological process. However, as he moved closer and closer to breaking out of the security trap, not only did his crisis mongering and brinksmanship progressively lessen, he dropped alcohol from his diet entirely.

Most stories end reasonably happily, if you wait long enough. This one is no exception. With a little help, he finally broke free and is now exploring those other dimensions that beckoned so alluringly. Having fought fiercely against burn out for a number of years, the healthiest solution for him was to exit the scene a few years before the "maximal retirement plan" would have dictated. Had he stayed, he might have come to resemble one of the other patterns of burn out that are described in the following section.

Styles of Burn Out

The "Dropout" style is the easiest to explain and the hardest to accept, for those who lament a talent drain from the field of administration. Dropouts simply say to themselves, "this is not for me" and leave. For a few, such a decision has come within days or weeks after accepting promotion to a management position. For example, a disenchanted nursing supervisor, finding it difficult to return to ward nursing at the same hospital, left for a nursing position elsewhere after experiencing one middle-management gathering. She was thoroughly dismayed by the seeming lack of concern evidenced for individual patients, some of whom she had come to know personally. Similarly, a minority physician who was elevated abruptly to the status of medical service chief took a few weeks longer to decide that he was helping neither his people nor himself in that role. Equally abruptly, he left for private practice in the city where he had grown up.

For most, however, the decision to drop out is preceded by months or even years of relative torment because "an administrator" is supposedly a highly desirable thing to be. Large organizations offer respectable and easy dropping out opportunities in the form of "staff" positions which exist outside of the administrative line. While they are respectable and require minimal risk taking, they seldom offer advancement potential equivalent to the line. This reality must be fully accepted if the change is to bring something better than a new breed of disappointment. Returning to a practitioner role in the same or another organization, as the nurse did, or to private practice, as the physician did, are solutions frequently chosen in the health field. Private practice has a particular allure for a number of administrative dropouts who discover that they don't want to be the boss, and they don't want to have one, either.

At the other extreme, a few drop all the way out; out of administration and out of their professional fields. Some drop out of white collar work altogether. A chief physical therapist took a year's leave of absence to go camping and three years later she was still building campfires in the wilderness between waitress jobs. One former government administrator is now running a bicycle shop. Another is earning a living as a writer. One case history in Chapter Five will describe a private-sector rehabilitation administrator who dropped out for awhile, but came back with renewed commitment to program building. This gifted individual would never have been lost to the world, but might have been lost to the field of administration had she not unlocked the secret of what had gone wrong with her work and her life.

Burnt-out administrators who do not drop out are more difficult for themselves and their associates than those who do. The classic pattern is illustrated by the "Impoverished Management" style alluded to earlier. This person shows low concern for both the goals of the organization and the people in it. High production and sound relationships are seen as in conflict, and the impoverished manager's major job is to stay out of the struggle. Problems are avoided or referred to others for solution. The impoverished manager keeps a closed mouth and expresses no dissent, avoids issues which might give rise to conflict by not discussing them with subordinates. Whatever creative ideas spring forth are seldom related to the job; they are more likely to concern outside interests. Any relationship between the work situation and/or supervisory actions and the flow of creative work from subordinates is denied.

Clearly, this describes a burnt-out individual who has dropped out in spirit if not in body. It is the result of an erosive process that happens to some administrators over a period of time—when they are threatened or disappointed by their roles and do not know how to correct this. It can happen rather quickly to a small number for whom the field was unsuitable to begin with. For most, however, such a state of collapsed ideals and practices reflects a relatively long and tortuous hike in the wrong direction wearing ill-fitted boots. The impoverished manager has also been called "The Do-Nothing Manager," as Harry S. Truman once called the Eightieth Congress. As must be brutally evident, having to work with or around one of these individuals is all the punishment any sinner ever required.

A less severe burn-out pattern which is frequently observed can be described in terms of another organization development tool: *The Life Orientation Survey* (Atkins and Katcher, 1971). The "LifO" also reveals certain changes which occur in management style when conditions turn from favorable to unfavorable. Individuals tested learn how their behavior alters under stress. They are scored twice on each of four scales reflecting the extent to which they are: supporting/giving, controlling/taking, conserving/holding, and adapting/dealing. The first set of scores show behavioral style under positive conditions; the second set, negative. A person who is highly supporting/giving when things are good may be less so under pressure. One who adheres tightly to a given set of principles when conditions are favorable may be ready to adapt and make whatever deals seem necessary when things get tough. An administrator who ordinarily acts as conservator may give away the store. A controlling manager may fling away the reins in disgust. Examples of changes in the opposite directions could equally well have been used because neither direction is considered inherently better or worse. A high score on conserving/holding, for example, may befit a comptroller very well but be less advantageous for an administrator in a program direction role. Rather, it is *change* from one's typical style, or the style used when conditions are favorable, which suggests that something may have gone wrong, if not outwardly, then inwardly. If such changes appear to be prolonged rather than a temporary reaction to a difficult time or situation, they may then signify burn out.

Most people, when they are unhappy, complain. Temporarily, it makes them feel better. The power of negative thinking to amplify their misery in the long run is blithely ignored in the face of immediate relief. This proclivity aids in the "diagnosis" of administrators who are in the process of burning out since being miserable, they tend to complain. To doubly complicate the matter, however, they don't always complain about what is burning them out because they don't always know. A sizable group are so out of touch with what is wrong that they translate their mental and spiritual discontents into bodily symptoms and then complain about those as if they were coincidental visitations. Psychologists call such people "somatizers."

Organizations under pressure are usually filled with burning-out somatizers; people with chronic headaches, frequent colds, and more seriously debilitating malaises. The vicious cycle of "feelin' bad" leads to neglect of healthful diet, exercise, and rest patterns, coupled with overuse of coffee, alcohol, uppers, downers, aspirin, antacids, cigarettes, and trash-food palliatives, leading to "feelin' worse." This goes around and around in ever tightening concentric circles until the victim is nearly strangled by them. Compulsive overeating to combat anxiety and depression result in weight gain which, in turn, contributes to more serious somatic disorders; and this is only one of many possible examples. A growing literature details the effects of stress, executive and otherwise, on bodily functions and even bodily structure. The relationships between stress and such disorders as hypertension, heart attacks, strokes, and even cancer, are ever more fully chronicled. Earlier in the post-Freudian era, "neurasthenia" was a very popular disease to have —or, at least, to diagnose. The cardinal symptoms are chronic fatigue, embellished usually by numerous other complaints, such as migrating aches and pains. It was considered a form of somatized anxiety, a disorder of psychogenic origin. The concept of direct psychogenesis of somatic disorders has largely disappeared as the intervening variables associated with stress become better understood. A syndrome which might have been labeled "neurasthenia" a couple of decades ago is now apt to be diagnosed as "hypoglycemia." The reason is: alterations in blood sugar level, the variable intervening between stressing events or lifestyle and the ensuing symptoms of fatigue (despite much rest and little exercise) and other "neurotic" indicators, has been documented. Whether labeled "neurasthenia" (which implies psychogenesis) or "hypoglycemia" (which implies somatogenesis) it requires a colluding interaction of psyche and soma to develop, and it is a frequent reaction to stress, chronic and acute. Practically speaking, for the burning-out administrator who needs his or her vitality to return and quickly, it hardly matters whether the chicken preceded the egg or vice versa. Somatic complications such as these may accompany an impoverished management style and be seen by the victim as the cause of it. This will probably not be an accurate perception. It is more likely that both are the reciprocating causes and effects of an underlying inability to flow with the stream of stressful events which life in the organization presents.

Two old and familiar stereotypes of impoverished managers are: the Company Man, and the Book Man. The former appears to have no guiding principles of his own, taking on those of the company or his immediate superior with ease. When the company comes under control changes and, therefore, philosophy shifts, this person can shift alliances and principles without apparent conflict. The Book Man, too, lacks inner guidance, but invests himself in a written manual rather than the more difficult-to-grasp polymorphous organization with its protean ways. Manual changes come slowly, and once they have occurred, they exist in black and white, requiring far less interpretation and judgment than "reading" a company. When people fitting one of these two stereotypes are discussed, it is usually assumed that this is their natural way of operating, and the impoverished nature of their styles is attributed to preexisting character deficits rather than to situational determiners. In some cases, however, it appears that Company Men (and Women) and Book Men (and Women) may be made, not born. In the face of overwhelming stress, people who began their administrative careers with far more creativity, individuality, and flexibility may retreat to the "safety" of applying others' standards instead of developing their own as situations arise. In short, the Company Man and the Book Man may be burn-out patterns rather than primary management styles. To the extent that characterological shortcomings are involved, lack of confidence in their own judgment interacts with stress to generate one of these two "retreating" coping mechanisms.

There is little positive to say about the Book Man. This style is so restrictive that it is dysfunctional in almost any management context, although it sometimes has value at technician levels. The Company Man, however, retreats less far and allows himself to deal at times with rapidly changing data. Viewed differently, this person may be the "new aquarian." The age of aquarius is said to be typified by a drawing back from absolutistic rights, wrongs, and allegiances. One way may be as good as another, and the individual who can get into the flow with whatever is there may be able to effect more gain than the more opinionated, determined soul who must try to force the universe to revolve his way. It is an interesting speculation, but one that history will have to evaluate.

In addition to these varying styles of partial or total burn out, there are isolated behaviors which also reveal a process of giving up the fight. Paying attention to these may forewarn and forearm administrators who suspect it is happening to them or to a colleague. Illustrative examples will be presented in the following section.

"Diagnostic" Signs

When a living organism perceives that its survival, safety, or security is threatened, it prepares to respond in one of two ways: fight, or take flight. As civilization advances, "survival," "safety," and "security" have come to mean far more than personal and genetic continuance. "Survival," for administrators, may also encompass the viability of programs and other "brain children" with which they identify. Thus, when threats to what one administers come along, one fights to protect them, or, if that seems impossible or excessively dangerous, "takes flight." "Taking flight" among humans is seldom the straightforward high-speed locomotion found among other species. Humans have learned less taxing, more dignified ways: denial, rationalization, turning off, dropping out, and other comparable forms of ignoring the problem and the pain it can cause.

When the threats and dangers perceived in the world become overwhelming, more and more does the organism opt for flight over fight. As the apparent odds for a successful fight drop lower and lower, the inclination to deny, ignore, or otherwise "fly" from the problem ascends. The conflict between competing urges to keep up the good fight versus renouncing it to run for cover constitutes the process of burn out—for administrators, practitioners, or anyone else. Burn out becomes a fait accompli when the struggle is over, and the person has settled into a regular pattern of opting for flight.

What are the clues to alert one that it is happening? Chronic complaining has already been mentioned as a cardinal sign. Complaining is a flight behavior, a passive substitute for fighting. Passivity itself is "diagnostic," and can be found at the core of many flight/burn out behaviors. In organizations, obstructionism is a familiar manifestation of what psychologists call "passive aggression." You "get" the other person by doing nothing—refusing to move yourself or something else out of the way. People who are burning out tend to feel progressively grumpier, and "getting" someone else once in a while begins to yield a perverse satisfaction. One pays in popularity, however. Obstructionists may come to be regarded as "paranoid" although their feelings of being disliked are in full accord with reality. Other aspects of perception do become distorted, and a resultant loss of objectivity is a frequent sign. Situations are perceived and responded to in ways which will minimize or reduce one's awareness of personal dissonance, regardless of what the facts would dictate to a less entangled observer.

Changes in lunch hour behavior are particularly revealing. "Last struggle" lunch hours may virtually disappear as the person fights to keep devotion to duty alive. As the struggle is given up, however, lunch hours may begin earlier and earlier, and extend later and later into the afternoon. The author observed one burning-out administrator as he altered his lunch-hour drinking from no alcohol, to one glass of wine with lunch, to one cocktail before plus one wine with, to two before plus two with, all in a period of ten months' time. He gained so much weight that he stopped drinking, but continued to burden his staff with irritability and an aura of gloom.

In some, an attitude of anarchism develops. Beaten down by the onslaught of too many balls to juggle, the person simply says, "To hell with it; let them fall where they may. The rules be damned!" Pari passu with this goes an element of nihilism; there is no point in trying to control destiny because first, it is impossible, and second, it really doesn't matter anyway. (This position sounds peculiarly close to the attitude of "unattachment" regarded as supremely wholesome by the current generation of Western interpreters of Eastern mysticism. The critical difference is that "nihilism" projects a desperate sense of loss, whereas "unattachment" reflects a joyous relinquishment of needs to control.)

Searching for another job is so unsubtle a sign that it could have passed without mention except for one thing. If someone you care for is looking for the same kind of job elsewhere and imagining it will be better because certain personalities will be left behind, it is important to point out that one very important person won't. The problem may lie within, or in the interaction between self and situational variables likely to be encountered in other management settings. Besides, personalities usually become unbearable only against an intolerable background. If the rest of the setting, and its match with oneself, is right, problem personalities can generally be tolerated with fairly good nature.

And speaking of good nature, its loss is the most telling sign of all. Specifically, the burnt-out individual loses the element of playfulness, the sense of fun, that can and must inhere in one's work, if stagnation is to be avoided. Work consumes a little less than half the waking hours of the average worker, and a little more than half for the average administrator. If work lacks the elements of play, good times, and plain, old-fashioned fun, the stultification will prove unendurable. Still another vicious cycle is created. Failure to see work as a source of fun leads to burn out, and burn out further impairs one's ability to have fun with the job. One of the administrators quoted in Chapter One summed up his chagrin by saying, "Frankly, it's just no fun anymore." No more pungent capsulization could be made of the burn-out experience.

This brings us to the end of this part of the chronicle, which has described the multifarious causes and effects of burn out among administrators. If this were all there were to the story, one could only expect the fires to glow ever more dimly until, at last, they were all burnt out. There is, however, another side to the story; one of hope, inner resources, and miraculously timed changes that are taking place in society today. These changes touch everyone, and have a very poignant effect on administrators. There is a definite stirring among the ashes, and Chapter Five unfolds a merrier tale.

Chapter 5

Out of the Ashes

Some administrators are highly resistant to burn out. They may be subjected to all of the same crazymaking situations as the others, but they somehow find ways to protect or renew themselves. What are those ways?

This final chapter begins with the stories of three veteran human service administrators who, at one time in each of their lives, appeared to have cashed in their chips and pulled out of the game. The three had very different reasons for their discontents, and their ways of pulling out were as varied as their reasons. Their ways of returning differed too, but one aspect was constant. Each returned with a renewed sense of purpose, revitalized reserves of energy, and an enhanced awareness of self which could protect them from the negative forces that had temporarily driven them away. All three have a great deal to teach others about recovering from the burn-out syndrome or, if it is not too late, avoiding it altogether.

Ray—The Bureaucrat Who Wouldn't Give In

Ray is the living, breathing proof that not all long-time bureaucrats fall into stereotyped ways, rigidified habit patterns, and unalterable expectations. Rather, generalization might lead one to conclude that they are among the world's feistiest fighters when a principle is at stake.

Ray served as the director of a large state's prison system for more than eight years. Appointed from within the ranks, he was soon to understand that a person in that position is not likely to please anyone. For eight years, he lived between the jaws of a rather ironic vise. Conservatives in the state thought he was intolerably liberal. Liberals thought he was implacably conservative. Both extremes were highly vocal, unlike the satisfied band of moderates in between. After his appointing governor left office, the new governor from the opposing party asked him to stay. He declined, saying it was a job for a young, ambitious, enthusiastic individual, which he no longer considered himself to be. He looked forward to working in his garden, bringing his elderly neighbors home-grown vegetables and doing needed household repairs for them, and going fishing whenever he chose.

His retirement did not last long. He had little desire to go fishing when he could go any time he chose; he missed the challenge of force-fitting it into an horrendous schedule. Moreover, he was too depressed to be very cheering to his neighbors. He was bored; he wanted something to administer. He let the governor know that he was again available, and an enormous problem to which he seemed the ideal solution was quickly identified.

The state's health department was headed by a physician prototypic of the individuals described earlier in the section titled "The Reblessed Professional and the Peter Principle." He needed help quickly and badly. Ray provided that help by serving as Chief Deputy to this Director for nearly two years—until the megalithic agency was reorganized into five smaller departments.

For a variety of reasons, Ray chose to postpone his second attempt at retirement for a few months. He accepted an assignment as Assistant Superintendent of the state women's prison to resolve certain problems there during his last tour of duty. Suddenly he noticed that he was having fun at work again. He tried to remember when he had felt this way before; eager to get up and go to it in the morning, pleasantly tired from a hard job well done at night, and overflowing with interest, energy, and creative ideas for problem solving during the day. An exerpt from a letter he wrote about two months after starting work there reads, ". . . haven't enjoyed myself more since leaving an institution fifteen years ago. Running prisons is really where my working heart is and I may not retire and [instead] continue . . . for awhile."

Ray had fully burnt out in top management, but because he had been there for so long, it never occurred to him to look elsewhere when he found he was not yet ready to retire. Only through an organizational accident did he rediscover that managing programs (middle management) was the real fun for him, not managing managers (top management) far from where the action is.

Many people, hearing that Ray had become an assistant superintendent of a single prison within the giant empire he had once directed wondered aloud, "How can his ego take it?" They believed they would feel demoted and dejected by such an apparent fall from power. What they did not reckon with is that to an inner-directed soul like Ray, such fanciful worries are not even issues. Returning to prison management, after the experience of directing the entire prison system, he saw only as a priceless opportunity to bring broadened vistas to bear on the job that was truly the love of his life.

"Don't stay too long in the same job," say the wonder course trainers, ". . . especially if the job is in top management. You should set out to accomplish a specific set of tasks, and if you haven't done it in five years, you won't in a lifetime." They don't say specifically where one is supposed to go after the five years have passed, but it is clear from the context that what is expected is *up. Sideways* is tolerable. In view of Ray's experience, it seems particularly tragic that no one has yet legitimized *down*. There are more reasons for this than face-saving ones. They have to do with improving the management of organizations.

An administrator with the experience of working at a high level in an organization can bring very special qualifications to a job at a lower level. Enhanced understanding of the total scope of the agency, problems in one unit which affect others, external forces which impinge on higher levels of management, the responsibility for supervising the same kind of position one now holds, and, very importantly, setting policy for the organization, all bring a uniquely expanded perspective to a top manager who returns to program management.

A related phenomenon has been pointed out in many health service professions when practitioners are first given supervisory responsibility. In a short while they notice that their professional skills have taken a quantum leap even though they have less time to practice their arts. Cliches such as "one learns best by teaching" become cliches only because there is so much repeatable truth in them. Universities are among the few settings where the model of a rotating administratorship is practiced in a paid-work setting. (It is also a common practice in voluntary organizations.) It is fashionable to detest having to serve as departmental chairperson, yet many who have done so admit that the experience was usefully broadening.

Ray is sufficiently sure of himself to joyfully bring such experiential resources to an assignment in the bowels of a leviathan department of which he was once the head. He can do so without wasting a gram of consciousness on such trivial worries as what others will think, how they will react, or doubts about what the change means in terms of his human worth. Hopefully, ways can be found to make it easier for others, too, to drop back in comfort to positions lower in the hierarchy when that could simultaneously save them from burning out and offer a boon to the organization.

Part of the problem, of course, is m-o-n-e-y. The higher you go, the more of it you get. (The universities are, again, an exception. Departmental chairpersons are more likely to be rewarded with slightly reduced teaching loads than with additional income.) Contrary to the supporting beliefs of the "money chic" ethic, money does not necessarily buy freedom. It frequently proves to be the tie that binds one to a painfully unsatisfying lifestyle. With that in mind, administrators who could take promotions without adjusting their spending habits to consume all of the additional income would be free, later on, to return to lower hierarchical levels if it turned out that the jobs down there were more fun for them.

John—Administration as Ministry

John ended his career by retiring from the position of managing president of a rather large vocational rehabilitation facility at the age of sixty-eight. He found it hard to let go, and the Board of Directors made it harder by annually rolling back the "mandatory" retirement age so he could work "just one more year" until they finally found someone who measured up in their eyes.

Like most other human service administrators, John began his career as a people helper; in this case, a circuit-rider minister and missionary. Although he gave up preaching for administration, in any reasonable sense of the phrase, John never gave up the ministry. He simply carried it out under an administrative title and by management rules. His clarity of purpose in this regard dissolved stresses that might otherwise have become problems.

Work was not always so idyllic for John; he burnt out too, for awhile. His way of manifesting it was typical of many human service administrators who, feeling unable to pursue their professional commitments, simply give up. In addition, his physical health suffered and proved a hard but effective way to learn about stress and how not to succumb to it. He learned his lessons so well that in later years he seemed unable to comprehend the meaning of "burn out." When perceptions are being shared regarding the exquisite frustrations confronting administrators, John's most frequent comment is, "Well, yes, I've seen that happen, but it doesn't bother me very much . . . that's just the way it is and you have to work around it."

And so it is and so you do, but many are less able to benignly acknowledge that fact. The Nisei generation has a phrase which approximates the spirit of John's acceptance of what is. In a rough rendering into arabic letters it is, "Shi ka ta ga nai." It means, again roughly, "If there is not a hell of a lot you can do about it, accept it!" It carries the connotation, "What else can you do?" A related principle is central to the martial arts. You don't meet force with force; you yield to your opponent's force and eventually use it to your own advantage. Although labeled "martial" arts, these disciplines train their practitioners to respond to all of life's exigencies with patient acceptance and utilization of what is occurring rather than reactive confrontation. This is what John's experience with burn out taught him to do.

Jacque—The Dropout Who Came Back

Jacque is a rehabilitation administrator of whom a critic once said, "When I go to visit her facility, she reminds me of a used car salesman who goes around kicking tires." He referred to the twin facts that she was extraordinarily aggressive and vocally proud of the programs she put together. Nonetheless, even her critics admitted that she was a topnotch administrator.

She entered the field of human services through nursing because she wanted to help people and that was a classic path for a woman to follow. She discovered soon that it was not a suitable field for her. Casting about for another way, she moved into rehabilitation counseling where her natural inclinations led her quickly into administration. Ultimately, she did what few rehabilitation administrators even conceived of at that time; she began building for-profit programs. Her success and her lifestyle escalated together until suddenly one day it was all over. A frightening experience forced her to look into herself and she disliked what she saw. She puts it something like this:

I stopped running long enough to look at my own motivations for doing what I was doing and I wasn't very pleased with what I saw. It wasn't at all clear that I was really doing anything to help anyone but myself and that wasn't working. Expensive clothes, a Porsche, and a high-rise apartment at the beach seemed to be more what it was all about, not any help I might be giving to other human beings. I decided that wasn't very good for me.

She concluded that she needed to get completely away from her work and then-current lifestyle in order to reassess her own priorities. She abandoned the fancy clothes and apartment, sold her Porsche, and used the proceeds to travel alone in the Far East for a year. She lived each day as it came, paying attention to every occurrence from which she might learn about herself. When she ended her travels, she concluded that she would never again work in a professional field. "Anyone capable of such impulsive actions could hardly be considered a reliable job risk!" She decided she could always get a job as a waitress, and that seemed okay. She was doing what she believed she had to do for her spiritual development, and how she earned enough money to survive was of secondary importance.

Despite her pessimism about her own employability, once it was known that Jacque was on the market again, she was destined never to become a waitress. The word was out, also, that she had undergone something of a personality transformation during the previous year. Many were eager to try to hire the "new" Jacque; others would have been perfectly satisfied to hire the "old." When she returned to professional work, the reactions of her former colleagues partially reveal the nature of the transformation that had taken place. The critic quoted earlier emerged from a momentary encounter with her exclaiming, "I can't believe that's the same woman I likened to a used car salesman ... she's so gentle, so serene ..." A woman colleague with whom she had often been compared mused in a half-whisper, "She seems so peaceful ... it makes me wonder if I am doing what I should with my life." In all situations, work related and other, she demonstrated consistently and clearly how effectively "A soft answer turneth away wrath."

It was not long before she ventured back into administration. In what has become accepted by her friends as the magical way in which things happen for Jacque, on the day following her decision to leave a job she had taken in Micronesia, she received an unsolicited invitation to come to work for a nationwide firm planning to build a new operation in Los Angeles. She met with her prospective employer and accepted the job. She was promoted before it began. In the course of initial planning meetings, she was judged to be what the firm needed for a higher position and was offered that one instead.

All of Jacque's decisions during the last five years have been made on the basis of her feelings and perceptions of what is right in terms of her spiritual development. None have been made in an effort to maximize her chances of succeeding, by whatever criteria, in her career. Yet her job success has been truly remarkable. Her jobs have steadily increased in the extent to which they offer the whole range of rewards cited earlier, plus one so rare it seldom makes the list; the opportunity for adventure. She is effective and strong. She takes care of business. She is the only woman in her firm in top management and is accepted without question by her all-male immediate subordinates. She is no spiritual day tripper. She is simply a person with a highly developed spirituality that contributes to making her whole life work. A phrase she sometimes uses best captures the essence of what has happened with her:

> You have to give it all up. You can't cheat and cling addictively to even one or two worldly attachments. But, if you *can* truly give it all up, it seems that somehow you get it all back!

Jacque's story shows that for some people it may be necessary to leave administration completely for awhile in order to gain a more balanced view of the causes of discontent and what to do about them. Her method was extreme. Others may also need to put distance between themselves and the sources of administrator burn out, but may find that less drastic measures can suffice. One approach that has been sampled by public administrators seems worthy of description because of its intriguing and unusual nature, and because it has not yet been reported elsewhere in the literature.

Wilderness Workshops

The experience of being alone is a stressful one for many people. The well-worn phrase "it's lonely at the top" attests to the fact that administrators feel their share of this particular type of stress. Skip Heck, an Arizona psychologist specializing in the problems of loneliness, points out that the compulsive work syndrome (perhaps more common among administrators than any other occupational group) is a frequent, though misguided, method chosen to combat loneliness. According to Heck, traditional methods of psychotherapy don't work any better to relieve the emptiness that lonely people describe than does lay advice to join groups and be with people more.

On seeing that being with others did not solve the problem, Heck came to believe that the solution lies not in avoiding isolation, but in bathing in it until it begins to feel good. This requires differentiating "loneliness," which connotes deprivation, from "solitude," which can be a self-nourishing and joyful experience. This new line of thinking led to his creation of the Wilderness Workshops. Here, people leave their everyday lives behind them and spend time simply experiencing how it feels to be alone in a peacefully beautiful environment. Even personal histories are left behind; no hot stamped university t-shirts or other mementos of "identity" are permitted. Discussion of life roles, status, and other aspects of personal history are almost taboo.

The workshops last for either three or seven days. The participants go together in a single vehicle to selected wilderness areas. On the way, they are asked to formulate three questions to which they would like to have answers. The questions may be as broadly philosophical or as narrowly mundane as the asker wishes. There is no focus whatsoever on personal problems or "hangups"; in fact, discussion of such is another taboo.

On the first day, participants pitch their tents in a circle around a campfire and alternate between times of silence and times of sharing the experiences they had in the silence. On the second day, they are told to "Go out and find a place that feels right to you." Some seek high ground while others gravitate to the terrain below, and Heck uses their choices of geography both "diagnostically" and "therapeutically" vis-à-vis a framework of Native American psychology. Central to the last is far greater emphasis on the commonalities and sameness of people, and far less emphasis on uniqueness and differences compared with "white man's" psychology. Heck also makes use of a system which describes four types of people in terms of their "perceptual gifts." The "buffalo" has the gift of seeing the world in terms of experience, the (largely external) events that take place. The "bear" has the gift of introspection. The "eagle" has the gift of seeing the world in broad vista, from a vantage point on high. The "mouse" has the gift of seeing the world from a close perspective and in detail. None is considered better than another; all four are needed.

Finally, Heck employs the observation that people tend to emphasize different sense modalities in their modes of responding. Figurative language provides clues to whether a person is responding in an auditory ("I *hear* you."), visual ("I can *see* your point."), or kinesthetic ("I can *dig* it.") mode. Also, he indicates that recent research into brain and language functions suggests that the direction in which one glances on being asked to think about a given topic also reveals one's predisposition to think in auditory, visual, or kinesthetic terms.

Putting these concepts together, Heck uses evidence from the participants' language and behavior to "diagnose" each one as a "visual eagle," "auditory mouse," "kinesthetic bear," or some other combination. Although everyone is given a "diagnostic label," it is a palatable one which can be used in the process of self-discovery during the remainder of the workshop, as the group continues to expand and contract, alternating between sharing and silence, aloneness and being together.

Heck describes a particular workshop he conducted for the director and division heads of a large human service agency. At the beginning, the boss was seen as relating primarily through memos and so busy with political and legislative matters that he wasn't available when his division heads needed him. After the workshop, the feedback received indicated that there was much more liking and sympathy for him, the others expressing understanding of how lonely it must be for him at the top. At the same time, the boss changed too. He stopped communicating through memos and made more time for his division heads.

Heck points out that the single, most talked about problem in organizations is communication. He asks, "When you have auditory mice, visual eagles, and kinesthetic buffalos trying to communicate with each other, but always in their own modes, how well can you expect them to understand each other?" He has found that when one person attempts to communicate in, say, an auditory mode, and the listener's comments reveal visual mode functioning, the two simply do not "connect." This is also true when one is speaking from a high-ground viewpoint and the other, from a low-ground perspective. He illustrated with a personal experience and described the help he received from a Navaho friend in dealing with it. Heck had complained that a member of his Board of Directors only wanted to talk about budgets while he (Heck) wanted to discuss programs. "He insists on being a mouse when I want to be an eagle!" he lamented. His friend's response was, "It is unfortunate that you are unable to see the world through his eyes. The fact that you can't is a lack in you. I hope you will be able to share his gift of perception." This helped Heck see the unproductiveness of putting down other people's different modes since all are needed. It might seem more comfortable if everyone's perceptual gifts were the same, but the world would be forever unenriched. Heck found he could easily slip into his board member's mode once the need to do so was clear and accepted, and that his workshop participants could do the same.

Unquestionably, administrative life could be more pleasant if the subtleties of communication misfires in organizations were clarified and corrected. Improvement should follow enhanced appreciation of the different ways of perceiving, thinking about, and responding to situations. How much more constructive and enjoyable it would be if the "old guard bureaucrats" and the "fresh blood political appointees" appreciated each others' different gifts of perception, and considered the inability to share them as something to be overcome rather than troublesome irritants to avoid.

Part of the importance of "getting away from it all," whether for a year of solitary travel in foreign lands or simply for a few days in the wilderness, is that it facilitates altering one's values when these are part of the problem. Currently, some rather significant value shifts are taking place in the whole of Western society that show promise of influencing decisions administrators make about their lives in a positive way. One of these is . . .

The Declining Addiction to Upward Mobility

A growing number of administrators are abandoning the struggle for one more promotion in an effort to make room in their lives for a new kind of quest. Promotional offers requiring transfers and consequent family disruption are being more frequently rejected. This is partly due to the increasing number of families in which both spouses have work ties, but that is not the sole determinant, since promotions simply requiring inordinate time and consciousness are being rejected as well. This withdrawal of investment from upward mobility and its promised enhancements of money, prestige, and power is a step toward freedom from fear (of an uncertain future) and addictive attachments (to whatever is seen as a means of controlling it).

Upward mobility is widely construed as an integral part of maintaining a tolerable degree of happiness in a power-oriented lifestyle. The virtue of the latter has generally been taken for granted since Alfred Adler popularized the striving for superiority over others as the prime motivator in human behavior. Ray, John, and Jacque have been able to jump off the treadmill of futile striving after this kind of power long enough to see that there is another way. The unnamed administrators who are turning down promotions which might disrupt less prestigious but more harmonious lifestyles have apparently caught a glimpse of the same thing.

Paradoxically, the decline in addiction to upward mobility may lead to greater enjoyment of whatever advancements do come. Ken Keyes, Jr. (*The Handbook to Higher Consciousness*, 1975), who advocates "upgrading" *addictions* (strong emotion-backed demands) to such things as security and power to *preferences* (nice but not necessary), illustrates how this happens in a passage elaborating on the phrase used by Jacque:

> One of the bonuses of higher consciousness is that when you give it all up, you get it all back. What you give up are your inner demands —what you get back is more of everything you need in order to be happy. As you grow into ... (higher) consciousness, you will find that you have all the power you need in your life—in fact you will have more than you need. For your unconditional acceptance of everyone around you will open doors that could never have been opened when you operated from ... (power-oriented) Consciousness.
>
> When you approach life with power addictions, you will be instantly resisted by the power addictions of other people. Instead of opening themselves to help you get what you want, they close themselves and are automatically antagonistic to your power thrusts which are threatening to them. As you grow into ... higher ... consciousness, you will begin to experience an effectiveness that you could never attain when you were shoving from ... (power-oriented consciousness), trying to bulldoze life into giving you what you thought you needed for happiness.

This may partly explain the remarkable success experienced by Jacque after she stopped striving for it. It may also be that the Zeitgeist is right for other administrators in other places to free themselves of the power and security addictions that are the root causes of burn out. The negative emotions generated by the disappearing rewards and sundry crazymakers described earlier can be seen in a new light, as nothing more than the automatic outcomes of such addictions.

Hand in hand with a declining addiction to upward mobil-

ity, there appears to be an accompanying tendency to re-
nounce the manipulative lifestyle and embrace one of greater
authenticity.

The Quest for Authenticity

A number of administrators who have declined
promotions related their decisions to a drive for
authenticity. One put it this way:

> I know without question that what I am doing now is real. I've been
> offered the job of assistant director but frankly, I have always
> thought we could do without that position. I don't want to take a
> job I see no need for just to make a couple thousand more than I'm
> getting now.

There are also signs of increasing desires for greater authenticity in the interpersonal relationships that exist among col-
legial peers. The now old-fashioned sensitivity training groups
were an early manifestation of this urge. Although their use has
largely passed, interpersonal authenticity building experiences
for work groups continue under other banners. George Bach,
who made artifice and subterfuge in courtship unfashionable
(Bach, 1969, and Bach and Deutsch, 1970), extended his marriage counseling techniques to the "marriages" which take place
in work organizations whether the partners say "I do" or not.
Being Bach's, it is a highly confrontative approach which can
nearly guarantee that survivors will learn to be more authentic
in their work relationships.

More and more, administrators are unflinchingly desig-
nating some portion of their budgets for "organization development," which typically includes some variant of authenticity-
building. The years have taught most O.D. consultants not to
encourage a level of intimacy which cannot be comfortably
sustained after the guided experience is over. Authenticity does
not require a high level of self-revelatory intimacy. One can be
authentic at many levels of closeness. Further, it does not

demand relinquishment of a private space; it implies only that one be honest about its existence and boundaries. Neither does it require abdicating authority. It suggests only looking honestly at one's motives and expectations when one "asks," "assigns," or "orders," and speaking forthrightly about what was observed. Some administrative decisions will always be arbitrary. Authenticity requires only that this be openly acknowledged and that external pressures not be feigned. "My hands are not tied; I made the decision and I'll stand (or fall) by it."

Administrators who have learned to present their ideas and motives honestly to peers, superiors, and subordinates are far less vulnerable to burn out because the intense pressures of maintaining a facade different from the felt reality are absent. When these pressures are removed, an accompanying palliative is allowed to emerge which provides an extremely important protection against organizational stress. It is . . .

A Sense of Play and Playfulness

Considering the fact that no one seems to know exactly what "play" is, there is remarkable agreement that it is vitally important to human growth, creativity, mental health, achievement, and countless other desirable human conditions. In the popular vernacular, play is often construed as the opposite of work. According to popularly known research findings, both classic and contemporary, that may be a reasonable polarization. Children and chimpanzees, at least, seem to abandon activities which are imbued with the stigma of work and to continue those left unstructured as play. In one sense then, work is activity with rules and play is activity which lacks them.

In a world with population so maldistributed as to cause severe human congestion in the centers where seventy-five percent of it lives, a proliferation of rules—laws, ordinances, regulations—could be expected as a means for keeping the swarming masses from accidentally trampling or intentionally murdering one another. And that is just what has happened, to the point where one's sense of freedom seems more threatened by the laws than by the swarming masses. Rules, remember, are what cause children and chimpanzees to drop out. Having sprung very recently from the former and, perhaps, remotely from the latter, we can assume that adult human beings may react similarly. Indeed, as more and more of life becomes "work"—legislated, coded, regulated, and monitored—we search ever more desperately for somewhere to play.

Burning-out administrators seem to have forgotten that their jobs don't have to be all work. They need to remember that their jobs can have elements of play and playfulness—their jobs can be fun—if they can only recapture the essence of doing what they do partly for the enjoyment of the process rather than solely for the necessity of the outcome.

The examples set by Ray, John, and Jacque, plus the hope-inspiring social value shifts described, offer some reassurance that protection or recovery from burn out is possible. In addition, there are some specific approaches which can be considered by readers interested in taking active steps. Most relate to developing the inner strength and resiliency required to withstand the pressures associated with administrative work and the system—putting them to work as catalysts to personal growth instead. Nonetheless, some of the system's errors are so utterly destructive (and at the same time appear to be amenable to change) that it would be foolish to ignore the possibility of correcting them. Therefore, several suggestions for "therapy" to the system are offered first.

If You Can, Change the System

The "security trap" appears to be the most pervasively troublesome of the system offenders, and the prospects for quickly altering the human tendency to quest after future financial security do not look favorable. The next best solution may reside in modifying the system so that security strivings will be less inclined to trap people in jobs they neither enjoy nor find suitable to their capabilities. At present, movement between the public and private sectors is severely penalized by retirement policies requiring so-many-years in service with a given organization in order to qualify for maximum benefits. Extending the concept behind the Public Employees' Retirement System (PERS) might be one fruitful method for alleviating the barrier.

PERS allows an individual to move from one sector of government employment into another while remaining within a single retirement system. If "reciprocity" is requested, all contributions made to the separate retirement programs are cumulatively credited to a solitary "years in service" criterion. This is, of course, an oversimplified description, as there are conditions, qualifications, and sometimes more than one benefit check involved. Also, uniformity of rules and benefits are not required. However, the basic principle does allow relatively unpenalized mobility among a greatly expanded array of job and career advancement opportunities.

It seems fully reasonable that the same concept might be extended to encompass private employment in both the nonprofit and for-profit sectors. Increased employee movement between the public and private sectors should yield some important additional benefits as well. First, one could expect enhanced understanding of the similarities and differences between the two types of work situations, alleviating the unrealistic envy or antipathy which are often found now. Second, the experiential enrichment which the greater variety of job and work setting exposure can provide should do much to combat the insular thinking which is fostered by staying too long in the same (type of) system. To expand the PERS concept to include essentially any employment which offers a retirement program would be a massive undertaking, requiring legislative groundwork. However, in view of the potential benefits, it seems worth an investigation of feasibility.

A second suggestion also relates to the problem of insular thinking. It is that "promotional only" hiring be sharply reduced and replaced by open hiring at all levels. This links closely with the first recommendation, in that a broadly encompassing "Employees' Retirement System" which encouraged greater movement among work settings would almost certainly be accompanied by increased hiring of agency outsiders at supervisory and management levels. This should help to create a freer, more regular flow of fresh ideas and approaches coming into an agency at policy-setting levels, and reduce the shock of outsiders' influences in the uppermost appointive positions. The fact is, people with experience working in a given organization should be at a distinct competitive advantage over outsiders who elect to apply. If they are not, then protecting them from competitors who, despite lack of comparable experience, show potential for performing better, looms highly questionable as a practice—if maximizing quality of service is the goal.

A third suggestion applies primarily to public sector agencies whose directors serve at the pleasure of elected officials. Planned reorganizations which involve two or more agencies often require an extensive approval mechanism which may even include the passage of enabling legislation. However, intra-agency reorganizations may often be carried out with no external evaluation of the necessity or soundness of the plan. The needless chaos this creates could be eliminated by a simple, two-part rule: that no major reorganization would be permitted within an agency during a director's first year of appointment; and after that, plans for reorganizing would require approval by the elected official. Such a rule could stem the tide of capricious "territory-marking" reorganizations and help to ensure that plans to redesign an agency's structure are based on careful analysis of functional needs. Naturally, there would have to be room for exceptions, as when a new director is brought in expressly to carry out a reorganization plan which has already been fully thought through and approved at higher levels. However, the principle is clear, and its explicit articulation should discourage impetuous reorganizing prompted more by idiosyncratic presumptions than knowledge of the actual needs.

The fourth suggestion is a call for intensive, comprehensive research into relationships between agency size, structure, and functions. Few would question that the trend toward consolidating into superagencies has created untold numbers of unmanageable nightmares. The evaluation of the experimental consolidation of local segments of two state agencies (see Chapter Two) revealed reasons why a full merger would probably not succeed. Despite apparently similar functions, the two agencies served different populations and together encompassed a far broader range of functions than any single administrator could be expected to manage competently. In addition, one agency had already grown too large to function with reasonable agility and would have increased its unwieldy bulk by seventeen percent.

The study described came about adventitiously, as a political face-saving maneuver, and chanced to yield some useful information. The time has come for similar studies to be initiated for better reasons. A few important questions which need answers are these. What are the optimal sizes of organizations devoted to (specified) missions? Are there maximal sizes beyond which it is counterproductive to go? How does optimal size relate to the geographic spread of an organization's installations and catchment area? What relationships exist between (specified) organizational functions and various structure/size combinations which might be tried?

The government and other gigantic, multilocation industries offer richly endowed laboratories in which to conduct controlled research permitting useful generalization. However, dwindling funds nearly always result in pulling all but the bare minimum away from research and pouring the existing resources into direct services. It is a myopic shame, because a few dollars invested in discovering what keeps organizations from functioning effectively might ultimately lead to government spending cuts (which taxpayers clamor for) without service cuts (which they decry). From casual observation of human service agencies which appear to "work" compared with those which don't, it would be easy to conclude that small must be beautiful. However, reducing agency size in a huge country with several very large states would be so difficult, and there are so many other variables which may produce the apparent relationships between effectiveness and size, that research corroboration is needed on this as well as the other questions.

A fifth and final suggestion is offered with tongue in cheek

—yet it may not be as whimsical as it sounds. Since administrators are being assaulted from one side by employee unions and by organized consumers on the other, and the two groups often appear to be at odds with the best interests of each other, why not exit gracefully and let them deal directly with one another on issues where the administrator is sure to be damed by one or the other for any decision made? When the employee-union and consumer-organization "bargaining teams" reach an agreed-upon plan of action, they could then come jointly to the administrator(s) with enhanced strength for their mutual position. This would be less threatening for the administrator, who would no longer fear attack by the other group if the plan were adopted. Staff support could be offered during their negotiations for such purposes as determining whether a proposed plan is in conformity with governing regulations (since both groups may have information gaps about legal constraints on policy decisions). However, administrative opinion and decisions would be held in abeyance until the teams complete their analyses, negotiations, and proposals.

This concludes the sampling of suggested system changes which might be contemplated as means of easing wear and tear on administrators. There are scores of more conventional (and, probably, more implementable) suggestions in the myriad available works on organization development and other matters managerial. At the same time, one even less conventional approach has been described which appears to work in the business sector to keep both administrative and sales personnel in tune with their needs so they can fulfill them in their work. It has been dubbed "New Age Business" and the question is . . .

Can "New Age Business" Come to Human Services?

The third issue of *New Realities*, a magazine devoted to holistic health and human potential reporting, carried an article titled "Consciousness in Business." It described the inner workings of a real estate firm which has allowed its founders to become millionaires in three years' time, and provides per capita earnings for its staff among the highest for any firm in the country. Clearly, it comes from the heart of the "money chic" ethic, but there is a noteworthy difference from outwardly similar modern businesses.

According to the *NR* article, the firm is doing business in a new way by creating an internal atmosphere supportive of "principles of the heart" which many people believe have been extracted from business. It self-consciously supports an ethical code embracing honesty, compassion, interpersonal support, and facilitation of staff success. It proposes to be a model for how a work organization can nurture personal growth as well as economic independence for its participants. Their approach to personnel selection is also atypical, relying heavily on intuitive processes. It was encapsulated as "Hiring 'winners' and letting them manifest their success here."

The *NR* reviewer is convinced that the process works because the working environment is a supportive family structure rather than an impersonal concatenation of policies regarding vacations, absenteeism, fringe benefits, temperature control, color schemes, and the presence of Muzak. The atmosphere of support is described as "intuitively palpable."

The article states that, theoretically, the same model could be applied to running a nursery school. Here, "Success . . . might be measured in terms of how happy the staff is, how much personal growth they experience, and how much the children gain as a result of exposure to such a positive environment." If true, it should be equally applicable to human service organizations generally. The goals, rules, rewards, and personnel will be different, but a model centering on good fellowship among colleagues should be singularly appropriate. Factors which could interfere with its adoption by existing agencies are legion, however.

For example, the article describes a small, single-location firm headed by the same individual who inspired the model in the first place. Moreover, all staff agree on their primary reason for being there; whatever else they want, they all want to make money. Thus, they face none of the problems associated with huge, multilocation organizations, and there are no People Helper versus Universe Tidier (see Chapter Two) motives to complicate the reward picture. Most important, they are free to hire whomever they wish without fear of later having to justify rejecting an applicant because "He or she didn't feel like a 'winner'" to a control agency.

"Principles of the heart" are being extracted from human service agencies, too—especially those grown large and politicized. Their erosion is clearly a contributor to burn out, as John's story illustrates. Therefore, it seems worthwhile to explore how the seven basic steps of the model might relate to human service organizations.

Step One: Define the purpose of the organization. This is not the same as its goals; it is the context in which they exist. It is on going and relates to the life and work satisfactions of the workers.

It may be difficult to convince human service workers that it is *okay* for them to build their own satisfactions right into an organization's statement of purpose. This may seem inappropriate for altruistically motivated helpers of people. In reality, of course, personal satisfactions are as important to people helpers as to anyone else, and to deny or downplay this constitutes a distortion of reality that may contribute to burn out. Jacque learned this the hard way when she discovered that her conscious denial of the importance of personal rewards had led her into a lifestyle of exaggerated, unconscious attention to them over which she was losing control.

Step Two: Define the "game" being played. The term "game" is used with no pejorative overtones or implications of unimportance to convey the sense of a specific endeavor guided by explicit rules, procedures, and goals. There is usually more than one being played at a time. For example, direct service staff and administrators have distinctly different endeavors and roles which must be clearly understood and must fit with the overall purpose while leading toward a common goal.

Step Three: Define the common goal. This must be a fixed goal to be achieved within a given time frame and must be broken down into subgoals to be accomplished within certain periods.

This should be the easiest of the seven steps for human service agencies, since many if not most have grown expert at management by objectives and zero-base budgeting. In the past, jokes ran rampant about "planning meetings to plan the planning." No one makes those jokes anymore. The phenomenon is taken for granted.

Step Four: Define the rewards for the participants on the successful attainment of the goal. At the time the goal is set, each worker should know what success will mean personally.

Again, the problem described in conjunction with step one arises. The reward for human service workers is often taken to be a sense of inner satisfaction that one has been helpful and nothing else is legitimately expected. (When, being human, we *do* expect more, feelings of shame may follow.) Human service practitioners and administrators must both acknowledge that it is okay, it is human, to want and expect more from their work.

Step Five: Establish the ground rules of the organization. Those of the firm described included: to be honest in communication, to keep agreements once they are made, to take responsibility for creating and supporting an abundant environment, to get off what clearly isn't working, to be willing to share and support so that everyone succeeds, to acknowledge others for what they have done, to choose and rechoose to be together, and to love.

These ground rules are more than examples; they are, in large measure, what the model actually is. Each is about as controversial as the golden rule, and may be equally hard to follow. Only one, however, presents specific problems for human service agencies. When the workers make no initial commitment to being together (as is almost always true in human service settings, especially in the public sector), it will not be easy for them to rechoose to be together again and again. Moreover, this is a high-risk philosophy which entails a continual readiness to go elsewhere. This may fit the temperaments of real estate sales people, but it may not fit those of human service workers. Actually, this is an issue the burning-out administrator needs to pay attention to, since a low risk-taking orientation causing one to stay physically in a situation one has mentally and spiritually chosen to leave can be a major factor in burn out.

Step Six: Workers define their personal goals for the same time period as for the organization's overall goal. The organization then agrees to support these. In the firm described, salaried people take one "goals day" off per month with full pay to work on their personal goals. Such an approach would not fare well in tax supported agencies, but other means of enacting the principle should be easy to identify once the concept is accepted.

Step Seven: Hire only workers who are willing to support the purpose, goals, and ground rules of the organization. Constantly examine and monitor the working environment, making sure that the organization and workers are in alignment. Be aware that each participant is working toward a greater sense of personal fulfillment and experience of abundance.

The first element of this step presents difficulties. Fair employment practice, equal employment opportunity, and affirmative action programs demand tight logic in the reasons given for rejecting an applicant. Phrases like "the person just didn't feel like a 'winner' to me" will not go over well at grievance hearings. However, to some extent, translating intuitive reactions into rational terms can be learned; and for those who have more freedom in personnel selection, assiduously following this step to the extent allowable can ease administrator wear and tear considerably.

This model focuses on changes in organizational procedures which can be tried in an effort to enhance the enjoyment administrators (and other workers) can get out of their work. At the same time, it suggests other issues relating to inner needs, values, feelings, and states that can be dealt with only by individuals. The remaining material will therefore be devoted to this other side of the equation—what administrators can do to protect themselves from the ravages of burn out when the system simply cannot be changed in significant ways.

If You Can't Change the System, Work on Yourself

A stepwise progression of investigation, decision making, and action is needed; and the material in this book can be used to guide the process. A quick review of the earlier chapters can aid in the detective work of uncovering not only the signs of burn out, but the particular form it is taking. Which crazymakers get to you the most? Your answer is a key to the kinds of addictions with which you will probably need to deal. Then it is necessary to take a little time out to re-assess priorities which have heretofore been taken for granted. These are the roots of a "decision tree," the trunk of which is diagnosing the needs for change. The earlier material in this chapter will be most useful for this stage of self-analysis. Next, it is time to plan a program for bringing about the changes which appear to be needed. Here, the tree culminates in a pro-fusion of interlocking branches. Do I get out? If so, to what kind of job do I go? Do I stay? If so, do I concentrate on reduc-ing the external sources of stress or the inner stress response? It is to questions such as these that the following material is ad-dressed, particularly, the alternative of finding ways to reduce the inner experience of stress.

The sixties gave rise to the human potential movement and it is alive, well, and growing. The seventies produced the holistic health movement, and the two are rapidly merging into a single conceptual entity. Its essence is total body-mind-spirit health in a self-actualizing person. A central concept is the devleopment of inner resources which allow one to "roll with the punches" or "flow with the tide." The common human tendency is to deny inevitability and try to force it to stop or go away. When the fates prove insurmountable, anger (at defeat) is added to pain (from the punch or big wave) and thus does misery in-crease. Burning-out people especially need to learn how to relax futile efforts to undo the past and control the future in order to have a little consciousness available to enjoy the here and now. "Let it be" has become the password into a new realm of living. It is reminiscent of the slogan employed for decades by Alco-holics Anonymous: "God grant me the courage to change what I can, the serenity to accept what I cannot change, and the wisdom to know the difference." It has been common knowl-edge for a long time that the inability to "let it be" can lead to alcoholism; now it is clear that it can destroy lives in countless other ways as well, including occupational burn out.

In a world grown technologically and organizationally complex, the possibilities for physical, interpersonal, and sys-

temological breakdown—with resultant stress on individuals—
have increased exponentially. The "system" is too immature to
guarantee against errors, yet too entrenched to make timely
changes expectable. There are so many places where something
can go wrong that correction takes longer than the victim can
endure if external change is relied on to end distress. The solution, obviously, is to turn inward for answers—and the multitudinous variants of the human potential/holistic health movement are designed for just this purpose. If you can't (yet)
change the system, work on yourself; develop the resiliency to
recoil, undaunted, from stresses which cannot be prevented
from occurring.

Keyes' (1975) earlier cited approach is among the most
explicit in this regard. Its enjoinder to "turn addictions into
preferences" is a straightforward (though difficult to achieve)
way of protecting oneself from damaging emotion when things
go wrong. If you are addicted to having the computer get your
number right every time, you will suffer when it doesn't. If you
prefer it, but are not addicted (have a strong emotion-backed
demand) to having it so, you can escape the anger that causes
suffering and simultaneously interferes with establishing communication with the humans in the system who will have to
undo the error for you. Keyes' training center has a number of
signs placed strategically about. One states, "You make yourself
and others suffer just as much when you take offense as when
you give offense." As the frustrations born of complexity multi-
ply, we are offended by both humans and machines ever more
frequently. As indignation mounts, we eventually become the
offenders. The effect is akin to a self-regulating machine on
positive feedback; it will destroy itself unless somebody pulls
the plug.

In learning to pull the plug, it is important to realize that
the crazymakers described earlier are crazymaking only if one is
addicted to having things happen differently. For example, if I
am addicted to hiring only those I see as the *most* competent
candidates for position vacancies, I will suffer when forced to
hire a less impressive candidate in order to undo past hiring
inequities—a goal to which I have no particular addiction. How-

ever, if I simply prefer it, I can say to myself, "This time I will be choosing a worker who will, first, help to correct inequities and, second, do a competent job of getting the work done. Although the first is not my cause célèbre, it is important and I can aid in its accomplishment." When preferences have replaced addictions, this is not done with cynicism or a sense of loss; nor is it one step closer to "letting the balls fall where they may." It is done with genuine and pacific acceptance of the fact that goals other than those personally held most dear may, indeed, be worthy of displacing one's own from time to time. After all, few administrators are totally without concern regarding inequities in hiring practices; it is simply a secondary goal which, accordingly, takes second place most of the time. Administrators who are not addicted to having their primary goals always take precedence can not only endure but can enjoy letting a secondary goal usurp primacy when the fates would have it so. It is still an accomplishment, and pleasure can be had from that if one is free to take it. Similar thinking could be applied to many of the frustrations which confront administrators.

Holistic health practitioners offer another approach. First, it must be recognized that one cannot hope to defend one's body-mind-spirit from the harsh and incessant stresses associated with administrative work unless one enjoys a reasonable degree of genuine health, or positive wellness. The traditional concept of the absence of an identifiable disease process is rejected as a definition of health. What, then, is it by a holistic characterization? A list of qualities ascribed to healthy people by two leading exponents in the field (Bloomfield and Kory, 1978) follows:

- trim and physically fit
- full of energy, vigorous, rarely tired
- free from minor complaints (e.g., indigestion, constipation, headaches, insomnia)
- alert, able to concentrate, clearheaded
- radiant, with clear skin, glossy hair, and sparkling eyes
- active and creative
- able to relax easily, free from worry and anxiety

- self-assured, confident, optimistic
- satisfied with work and the direction of their lives
- able to assert themselves, stand up for their rights
- satisfied with their sexual relationships
- free from destructive health habits, particularly smoking, over-eating, and excessive drinking
- fulfilled and at peace with themselves

These are not construed as the characteristics of an elite group at the upper end of the normal distribution. They describe what average people should be able to expect if they take reasonable care of themselves. "Reasonable care" means that attention is paid to habitual behaviors that can build or destroy health. Good nutrition, adequate rest, sleep, and relaxation patterns, abstention from tobacco, moderation in eating and drinking, regular exercise, and—very importantly—a balanced state of consciousness must be maintained.

What makes the holistic approach to health care particularly relevant to administrators, with their unending need to cope with surprises, is that it places central emphasis on the role of stress—to the physical, mental, and spiritual aspects of one's being—in the undermining of health. Accordingly, its practices focus on ways to lessen the impact of stresses on individuals.

With respect to maintaining a balanced state of consciousness, some variant of meditational practice is frequently recommended as a regular part of daily life. The potential value of this is fairly well accepted within the field of administration. A surprising number of organizations have provided meditation training, usually in Transcendental Meditation (TM) techniques, to administrative and other staff through in-service training or organization development programs. One occasionally hears of an administrator who has personally experienced benefit from other Eastern approaches, such as yoga or the martial arts, urging colleagues to explore them too—to create or restore balance to their harried lives. Oddly, less consideration may have been given to more conventional approaches in programs designed to help administrators deal with stress. However, relaxation training is frequently used, and a few exercise programs have been instituted in response to concern about executive heart attacks. (Diagnostic of the problem, perhaps; they often involve competitive sports!)

The health of one's body-mind-spirit can be affected by efforts aimed at any of its three aspects. Although improving one's nutrition would seem to be a "body" approach, it is well known to yield benefits to mood (a "mind" state) as well. Similarly, many people report that their physical strength and energy are greatly improved by following such "mind" approaches as meditational practice. While body and mind have been rather well attended to, spirit has been largely deleted from the equation. The author knows of no programs designed for administrators which emphasize spiritual approaches. Even the "Executive Stress Management Training" workshop offered by the Himalayan International Institute for Yoga Science and Philosophy—an organization devoted primarily to spiritual concerns—is described in their advertising literature in terms avoiding spiritual reference. "Exercises for keeping the body flexible . . . decreasing muscle tension with systematic relaxation techniques . . . regulation of breathing processes" are explicitly mentioned. It is as if administrators are seen as hard driving, practical people who would not have much patience with any of the spiritual stuff. And yet, it is very likely that numerous instances of burn out among administrators reflect "spiritual crises," nonpsychopathological episodes wherein individuals become painfully uncertain about the purpose and meaning of their lives' directions. Here, attention to mind and body can undoubtedly help, but more direct attention to matters of the spirit might be more effective.

For individuals interested in pursuing the maximization of their health and human potential, an infinite choice of paths is available. The core of most, from aikido and biofeedback to yoga and Zen, is learning to stay calm and "centered" in the face of stress. However, the holistic health and human potential movement(s) are not the only ones which have significant contributions to make in the campaign against administrator burn out. The self-help movement, which dates back at least to the inception of Alcoholics Anonymous, is currently experiencing a remarkable growth spurt. This burgeoning movement has also made its contribution, as will be seen below.

"Adminanon"

A group of health service administrators were relaxing one evening at dinner after a particularly difficult day of interagency negotiations. It seemed as though the "best interests" of each agency were somehow orthogonal to those of every other. As a result, several carafes of house wine were required to put the group in a sufficiently relaxed mood to make a convivial end of the day possible. The conversation which ensued produced a number of conceptualizations which are relevant to the matter of administrator burn out and what can be done to "treat" the victim. The discussion began when one weary soul asked if any of the others would like to join a new self-help group he had just decided to establish: "Adminanon." The nature of the organization was immediately clear from its title, an obvious contraction of "Administrators Anonymous." Here, administrators who felt that administration was taking over their lives and jeopardizing their health, happiness, and marriages could seek help from others like themselves who would understand. The group, lubricated by a very adequate little Cabernet, proceeded to develop the ground rules and programs they considered appropriate for such an organization.

There was general agreement that applicants should not be required to go "cold turkey," abandon administrative work entirely, in order to join. It was recognized, however, that this might prove to be the best or only solution for some members. Most to be hoped for was that, through the support of the group, members would find that they could continue administering programs forty hours per week (no more) without developing a toxic condition from the activity. An example of a toxic condition which comes about is finding that one cannot *stop* administering during the remaining 128 hours of the week. The ability of certain former alcoholics to engage, safely, in social drinking, and of some heroin users to partake of weekend "chipping" without becoming full-time addicts were cited as evidence that such was a reasonable goal.

One person had just read Baba Ram Dass' *Be Here Now* (1971) and opined that "Be Here Now" should be the slogan of the organization. "Clearly," he said, "the failure to experience fully what is here right now, because of preoccupations with events of the past, future, and elsewhere, is a major contributor to burn out." He felt this was particularly true for administrators, whose concerns for precedents (past) and planning (future) wrench them continuously away from the present. Another, who had recently finished Carlos Casteneda's *Tales of Power* (1974), countered that "Stop the Inner Dialog," while similar in intent, would be even more to the point for administrators. He reasoned that a major cause of their failure to appreciate the here and now is a tendency to ruminate continually upon the conflicts, problems, pressures, and demands which besiege them. If this negatively reinforcing inner recitation could be stopped, so, too, might the process of burn out be abated. In other words, he felt that what they need is to inwardly shut up. A third had paid a recent visit to the Living Love Center in Berkeley to talk with Ken Keyes. She believed the slogan should encapsulate Keyes' differentiation of "enjoyable games" from "real happiness." Her reasoning was that administrators may get hooked on winning such things as favorable policy decisions and funding, which enable them to expand the range of enjoyable games they can play. These, however, have nothing to do with true human happiness, which seems to come more readily to people who have given up attachment to games altogether. A fourth passed the carafe and soon after, it was agreed that the organization could have unlimited slogans, and contributors would be encouraged to provide them in woodcarved or illuminated-scroll editions.

Such details having been taken care of, the discussion turned to programs. A "diagnostic clinic" would be the initial phase, followed by a two-track program borrowing concepts from the field of marriage counseling. This was considered singularly appropriate in view of the strong sentiments of the group that they were "married," both to their jobs and to certain of their colleagues; and a number of those "marriages" were on the rocks. Depending on the "diagnostic" findings, members would be routed to either the "Reconciliation Counseling" or "Creative Divorce" track. Candidates for "Reconciliation Counseling" would be those who might or might not need a "trial separation" (similar to a "rest cure," in other parlance), but who would be expected to return to administer another day. All present agreed that one of the most important program components would be counseling to help administrators deal with their needs for approval and their anxieties about being considered "bad guys." Candidates for "Creative Divorce" would be those who were either irreparably burnt out, or who were never suited to administrative work in the first place. At this point, the conversation took an interesting philosophical turn.

Just as divorce, in its more usual context, is no longer deemed certain evidence of failure but, rather, a simple indication of legitimate growth in different directions, divorce from administration was described similarly. The group tended to agree that while it may serve one's psychological growth needs well during a given phase of life, it may outlive its usefulness. However, because of the human tendency to settle into lifestyle routines which are hard to break, especially when society says one has "arrived," we fail to attend to the signs that the time has come to move on. One participant cited a specific situation relating to this concept; she rinsed her mouth with Cabernet and delivered the following oratory:

> For all the inanities of the public system, one element is pure rationality. That is the four-year term of office. Somehow, the founding fathers sensed just how long it takes to burn out in a high-level job. Everyone knows you should not stay in a top management job more than five years because you can't keep up the head of steam needed any longer than that. The founding fathers knew it 200 years ago, they just cut it a year closer. This *should* give a clue to administrators who complain about feeling burnt out after fourteen years in the same job. Maybe the problem isn't what they think. Maybe the problem is letting their security needs lock them into situations the founding fathers could have told them 200 years ago would be hazardous to their health. There may be only one solution, and it's

not psychotherapy. It is to get out, start truckin', leave the retirement funds in a deferred account, and go find another job that doesn't hurt.

The following day, when the group reassembled for continuing negotiations, one remarked that he felt better than he deserved to considering the amount of wine consumed the night before. The ice thus broken, several others joined in with similar observations. They had awakened, cautiously opened an eye to lessen the impact of daylight, and realized with surprise that they felt just fine. The experiences ranged from relief to exuberance, but all were positive. As the sharing progressed, it became evident that the discussion of the prior evening had had a remarkably therapeutic effect on all concerned. They noted that it had not been the usual grousing session wherein people compete for air time to voice their complaints and pay for the chance to ventilate by listening quietly (though inattentively) while others take their turns and by murmuring sympathetic responses on the order of "Yeah, it's tough."

Instead, they had mined beneath this level of superficial relief and come across some nuggets of genuine understanding of the roles they played in creating their own unease. And they found they were neither fools nor alone. The camaraderie generated in this process of sharing carried over into the interagency negotiations during the day. Although the meeting was scheduled to last until three o'clock in the afternoon, the work was completed by one-thirty. The orthogonality of their interests had dissipated, and "compromises" which compromised no one were arrived at with relative ease. As they gathered their materials to leave, one member of the group remarked, "I think 'Adminanon' has just had its first session—and I think it worked!"

Reassessing Power

Speculators on the human condition are fond of noting that at one time, in the days of the landed gentry, power equaled *land*. Now, they say, power equals *infor-*

mation. Whoever has the critical information makes the "score." For this reason, information which should belong to the community of humankind is jealously guarded for the power advantages it can yield its possessor. Since the basis of power is transmitted (shared) by a process known as "communication," it is no wonder that communication is seen as the single largest problem in organizations. There are at least as many forces operating against effective information sharing as for it. To ask for clearer and fuller communication may be tantamount to asking the duke or the peasant farmer to turn over a bit of his land for some worthy purpose. A sensible person would not expect it to happen unless good assurances and incentives were offered.

The psychological establishment has convinced us that "statistically normal" means "healthy." Therefore, when catastrophe strikes and someone blandly says, "Oh, okay," and goes on about their business, we are apt to say, "That person is nuts. It is *inappropriate* not to suffer under such circumstances." The wall plaque frequently seen in office settings that proclaims, "If you can keep your head, while all around you, folks are losing theirs, then you obviously don't understand the situation!" attests to this fact. We tend to reject the possibility that people who remain undaunted in the face of presumably upsetting circumstance represent the "supersane" tail of the normal distribution. We assume, instead, that they are out of touch with reality. It is time to reconsider this defensive prejudice.

In recent days, there appears to be a fledgling recognition that the kind of power derived from possessing either land or information may not be altogether worth having. Another kind of power is being rediscovered which works better. It also feels better. This is the power which attends freedom from mundane attachments. If you are ready and able to amiably accept any outcome of any situation, you are powerful indeed. No one can hurt, frighten, or irritate you; you are invincible—and it all comes from within. The facts of the eternal world (such as losses of funding, demotions, or worse) have no power over the quality of your mood.

Keyes' statement regarding what power is and isn't puts it

very well. The kinds of power strivings associated with the accumulation of land or the guarding of information arouse counterstrivings in others which will ultimately undermine one's own base of power. On the other hand, the kind of power which emanates from "giving it all up," renouncing attachment (addiction) to particular objects and outcomes, is invulnerable to external attack. Now that is power! His basic message is, "Stop manipulating and bulldozing people into doing what you think you want, and start doing what you have to do to magnetically attract them." The philosophy behind participative management theory says the same thing, but only describes the outer shell of what should occur; it does not attend to the inner states managers must attain in order to create a climate of genuine participation. Without this, participative management (power sharing) efforts often deteriorate into manipulative pretense, not unlike the so-called progressive educators who, earlier in the century, simply manipulated their students into believing they had a voice in determining subject matter and methods of study in order to secure cooperation with a preplanned curriculum. Truly participative management can be engaged in only by people who are free from addictions to having their own way; otherwise, "participation" becomes a sham.

The essence of the matter is that power over others, in the absence of power over oneself, is vacuous. "Power over onself" should not be construed as the exertion of controls over impulses, or will power, as it might be by people who have not yet glimpsed the awesome power of being truly free from dependencies on external conditions for their happiness. Power is, rather, a form of freedom; freedom to stay or go, freedom from traps which hold others in their jaws. Very importantly, it is freedom from binding attachments which appear to be external, and are treated as if they were, but in fact reside within. A dramatic illustration of this was provided one day, not by a human, but by a Springer spaniel.

Peggy, as her owners called her, could easily be controlled by placing an unanchored leash across her neck. When she felt the weight of the leather thong, she appeared to assume that she was tied. She made no efforts to leap up, pull against her constraints, or even move. She lay quietly, looking forlornly at her "captors," and waited to be "released." When the leash was removed, she bounded into frolicsome action, seemingly delighted that she had been "freed." Once, the leash was laid across her neck and the experimenting humans walked away. Peggy moaned piteously, as if begging them to remember the condition in which they had left her. Although they remained out of sight for several minutes, Peggy made no effort to get up. She was convinced she was tied and no efforts of her own would free her; she would have to await the actions of the group. Her owners had never intentionally conditioned her to respond in this manner and were perplexed as to how it had happened. How often this enactment comes to mind when the behavior of people in organizations is being observed! The only power Peggy needed was knowing that she was free; the corollary is obvious.

Although a single word, "power," is used, it is clear that it denotes two very different phenomena. One might be termed "coercive power" ("push power"). This is the kind associated with such concepts as "authority," "rank," and "clout." It is also associated with power-oriented consciousness and the suffering that accompanies cyclical victory and defeat. The other might be termed "magnetic power" ("pull power"). This is the kind associated with true leadership, as opposed to mere "power holding" or dictatorship. The true leader is the one who keeps in touch with the needs and desires of followers (subordinates) so that policy directions will be in keeping with that reality. The power holder (autocratic leader) attempts to squelch or ignore those needs and wants, lest they interfere with a preformulated agenda. These are the souls who become most lonely at the top because they won't let down their hair to allow rescuers to climb in.

Just as health qua absence of illness is no longer viewed as sufficient and the concept of positive wellness is coming into use, so may there be a revolution coming regarding "sanity." The absence of blatant mental-emotional dysfunction is not sufficient grounds for assuming a state of sanity because it allows for such "insane" behavior as attributing lack of suffering to pathological causes. People who exceed normal expectations for coping with life's exigencies and can be joyfully constructive through them all are coming to be referred to as "supersane"—showing "sane" to be the humdrum quality we always thought it was. Abjuring mediocrity, many insist they would rather be crazy and interesting than an average bore. The other tail of the distribution is available for occupancy, however, so one could aim for becoming a member of the supersane minority instead.

Supersane people were cited earlier (see Chapter Three) in the context of "accidental empire builders." Part of the magic is their enjoyment of the *process* (what is here, right now, for sure) rather than seeing it as a necessary but evil hurdle between them and some future, uncertain fait accompli. The latter attitude generates days, weeks, months, or years of sacrificial effort for a moment of pleasure when it is finally over. The former offers enjoyment for the whole time. The supersane do not suffer just because everyone else they know, under similar circumstances, would. They can say, "I blew it," or "I lost that round," and walk away as jauntily as they came because their happiness is not dependent on such outcomes and they know it. That knowledge gives them power—the power to build and break apart, succeed and fail, win and lose, with equal equanimity.

It seems to be the quality of equanimity which attracts the following, the cooperation, the trust of others. With some people, no words are needed to convey the fact that others need never fear a "stab in the back." When trust is fully justified, this is usually intuitively palpable. Administrators who sense they are not trusted should search within before musing on the etiology of their colleagues' paranoia. If the question, "Might I give in to their adversaries' eleventh hour pleadings?" yields an answer of "maybe . . .", then the lack of trust has some foundation, even though the breach would come—not from self-serving machinations—but from a simple failure of data processing. The supersane make few such mistakes. Because their consciousness is free from the distractions besetting the merely sane, it is available to ensure that failures to consider such contingencies during pressured situations seldom occur. This, along with the other qualities described, gives the supersane administrator remarkable power which requires no guarding whatsoever; it is just there.

The administrator who knows what real power is and where it comes from will be insulated against burn out. Burn out appears to be a function of the distance between expectations and actuality. The supersane administrator maintains a narrow gap between the two. In the absence of addictions to an idealized image of the way things should be, reality offers few rude surprises. Rewards don't disappear because they issue from within, regardless of fluctuating external circumstance. Neither the system nor the people can make supersane administrators crazy. They accept what is and do what they do in full recognition that their efforts could fail—at least they had fun getting there. They may choose to leave a job if the enjoyment becomes diminished, but not because they are burnt out. They would have made their move as soon as they sensed it could happen if they stayed longer. Thus, the supersane administrator is in touch with an inner guidance system which will give explicit directions, on time, to anyone who would pay attention.

Adler may have been right, that humans strive for superiority, power over others; but perhaps that can be viewed as a developmental phase. Jung may also be right, that humans can progress beyond this level of need, "put it away with other childish things," and ascend to a higher level. Once the coercive power strivings which lead some of us to enter and climb administrative hierarchies are "put away," the magnetic powers at last have a chance to appear. There can be no bargaining ("If I give up this coercive power striving, I get this bigger kind"). You truly have to give it all up. You will know when you have, because you will note that you are beginning to get it all back.

Bibliography

Atkins, Stuart, and Katcher, Allan. *The Life Orientation Survey*. Beverly Hills: LifO Associates, 1971.

Bach, George. *The Intimate Enemy*. New York: Morrow, 1969.

Bach, George R., and Deutsch, Ronald M. *Pairing*. New York: P. H. Wyden, 1970.

Bloomfield, Harold H., and Kory, Robert B. *The Holistic Way to Health and Happiness*. New York: Simon and Schuster, 1978.

Brown, David F. "Consciousness in Business," *New Realities*, Vol. 1, No. 3. 1978.

Casteneda, Carlos. *Tales of Power*. New York: Simon and Schuster, 1974.

Hall, Jay, and Williams, Martha S. *The Styles of Leadership Survey*. Los Angeles: Teleometrics, 1968.

Hawken, Paul. *The Magic of Findhorn*. New York: Harper and Row, 1975.

Kemp, Bryan J., Personal communication, 1977.

Keyes, Ken, Jr. *The Handbook to Higher Consciousness*. Berkeley: Living Love Center, 1975.

Maslach, Christina. "Burned Out," *Human Behavior*, Sept. 1976.

Mercerier, Darlene King. "Why State Government Fires So Few Incompetents," *The California Journal*, Dec. 1977.

Peter, Laurence J. "The Satisfaction of Opting for Simplicity," *Human Behavior*, Aug. 1978.

Peter, Laurence J. *The Peter Principle.* New York: Morrow, 1969.

Ram Dass, Baba. *Be Here Now.* San Cristobal: Lama Foundation, 1971.

Richter, Curt P. "On the Phenomenon of Sudden Death in Animals and Man," *Psychosomatic Medicine*, May–June, 1957.

Roberts, David C. et al. *Co-location of Employment and Rehabilitation Services: An Experiment as a Conflict Resolution Strategy*, Final report of demonstration grant 12-P-57712, Office of Research and Demonstrations, Rehabilitation Services Administration, Office of Human Development, DHEW, Washington, D.C., 1977.

Shubin, Seymour. "Burn Out: The Professional Hazard You Face in Nursing," *Nursing '78*, Jul. 1978.

Skinner, B. F. *Beyond Freedom and Dignity.* New York: Knopf, 1971.

Warmath, Charles F., and Shelton, John L. "The Ultimate Disappointment: The Burned-Out Counselor," *Pers. and Guid. J.*, Vol. 55, No. 4. 1976.

Watts, Alan. *The Wisdom of Insecurity.* New York: Pantheon, 1951.

Index

Accountability, 17, 19-22
Addiction, 101
  to own biochemistry, 66, 67
  vs. preference, 89-90, 102, 103
Adler, Alfred, 88-89, 114
"Adminanon," 106-109
Affirmative action, 9, 10-12, 44
Appointive positions, effect of on
  lower-level workers, 9, 29-30
Body-mind-spirit, 101, 105
Book Man (Woman), 72-73
Bureaucrat vs. revolutionary, 43-46
Centralization and control, 35-37
Changing oneself, 100-106
Charismatic leaders, 44, 47-48
Civil service, 16, 26
Communication, 63-64, 87, 110
Company Man (Woman), 72-73
Consumers, 12, 13-15, 32-33, 44,
  61
  and unions in negotiations, 95-96

Control agencies, 7, 18-19, 22
Country Club Management, 64
Crass Materialists, 52-53
Decentralization, 36, 37
Do-Nothing Manager, 70
Dropout, 3, 68-70, 82
Empire Builders, 32, 41, 42-43
Equal employment, 10, 16, 43
Executive Stress Management
  Training, 105
Fight or flight response, 73-74
Future money, 24, 25, 26
Giving it all up, 84, 89, 111,
  114
Good Old Boys, 62, 63
  as administrators, 53-57
Heck, Skip, 85-88
Higher consciousness, 89-90
High risk takers, 28, 66
Holistic health movement, 96, 101,
  102, 103, 104, 105

Human potential movement, 101, 102, 105

Impoverished Management, 64, 67 69

Jacque (case example), 82-85, 88, 92, 98

John (case example), 81-82, 88, 92

Juggler, 59-64

Jung, C. G., 114

Keyes, Ken, Jr., 89, 102, 107, 110-111

Law of reverse effort, 24, 65

"Let it be," 101

Low risk takers, 27, 28

Malicious compliance, 18

Mergers, 32-35, 94-95

Middle managers, 1, 17, 38, 43, 79

Middle of the Road Management, 64

Minorities as administrators, 53-57
  and ethnicity, 55
  vs. Good Old Boys, 56

Native American psychology vs. "white man's," 86-88

"New Age Business," 96-100

Opportunity
  for creative expression, 6, 25
  for promotion, 6
  to deal directly with people, 61-62

Participatory management, 18-19, 111

Passive aggression, 74

People helpers, 1, 48, 49, 50, 52-53, 81, 98

Peter Principle, 48, 52

Power, 5, 18, 49
  as freedom, 111-112
  coercive vs. magnetic, 112
  of the external world, 110
  over oneself, 111

reassessing, 109-114

Promotion, 27, 49

"Promotional only" jobs, 26, 28, 29, 93-94

Public Employees' Retirement System (PERS), 93

Ray (case example), 78-81, 88, 92

Reblessed professionals, 48-52

Reorganization, 30-32, 43, 94

Retirement programs, 24, 25

Reverse discrimination, 12

Revolutionary, 41
  vs. bureaucrat, 43-46

Risk taking, 42, 68, 99

Security, 6, 24-26
  trap, 66, 92-93

Self-help movement, 105-106

Selye, Hans, 66

Sense of play, 75, 91-92

Spiritual development, 83, 84

Stress, 66, 70, 71, 72, 81, 101, 102, 103, 104

Supersane, 43, 110, 112-114

Task Management, 64

Team Management, 64

Teamwork, 15-17, 46

Uniformity of service and standards, 37-39, 45

Unions, 6, 7, 8, 65
  and consumers in negotiations, 95-96

Universe Tidiers, 32, 33, 52-53

Upward mobility, 88-90

Value of moving down, 80

Women as administrators, 53-57
  and femininity, 55, 56
  and other women, 56
  response to, by subordinates, 55
  treatment of, by superiors, 62
  vs. Good Old Boys, 56